PRINT EDITION

Forbidden © 2015 by Matthew Freake and Mirror World Publishing

Edited by: Markus McDaniel

All Rights Reserved.

*This book is a work of fiction. All of the characters, organizations and events portrayed in this novel are either products of the authors' imagination or are used fictitiously. Any resemblance to actual locales, events or persons is entirely coincidental.

Mirror World Publishing
Windsor, Ontario
www.mirrorworldpublishing.com
info@mirrorworldpublishing.com

ISBN: 978-0-9920490-6-5

For Ruthanne

Forbidden

Matthew Freake

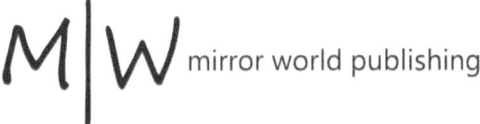

Prologue

His eyes hurt from staring at the computer screen all day. He was so close to finishing that he ignored the pain in his eyes and the pain in his heart. He had to finish the book. His home office was small and the glow from the monitor caused the walls to glow blue; the same colour that reflected on his face as he typed. The one window in the room showed the large oak tree that encased most of his small backyard.

He stopped typing. He was finished, finally. Pausing a moment to read what he had just written, he moved the cursor up to the top of the screen, clicked on save, and then turned the monitor off. He sat back and felt accomplished. It had hurt, reliving all of those memories, both the good as well as the bad, but he was glad he had gone through with it.

He wiped away the single tear falling down his cheek and smiled. He was happy. He knew in his heart that Alex would have been happy as well.

"I miss you, Alex," he said, standing up. He moved his office chair, turned away from the computer and left the room, leaving all of the memories contained within it.

The only man I ever loved is dead. This is our story...

Chapter One

It happened a long time ago; 1957 was the year. The war was over and it was supposed to be a time of love, peace and friendship. And, for the most part, it was. The summer had just begun and I was still a child in many ways; fresh out of school, but ready to take on the world.

Before I went on my world adventure into manhood, I heard about a job constructing a new railroad that went from Sydney, Nova Scotia all the way through to Vancouver, British Columbia. I thought, *what an opportunity to be a part of history!* Apparently, everyone else felt the same way, because when I arrived at the compound there were at least a hundred people already there.

The rail yard was old, well, at least the buildings that made up the compound were old. The ground was mainly dirt with a few patches of grass, primarily around the bases of the buildings. Normally the dirt there was hard, except for that day, because it had rained earlier. Everything was muddy with puddles situated in tire tracks left behind by passing trucks.

The cabins were scattered in rows and one of the larger buildings had a bench out front with five or six cloth sacks resting on top. Those sacks were filled with towels and clothing and each bag was numbered with the number of a coordinating cabin, which was something I would come to learn in my first few days. This was home for the next three months.

I was in line to register with my best friend, James. He was about five foot, seven inches with dark brown hair and his eyes were so dark you could not tell where his pupils were. He and I had attended school together since we were seven years old. We had always been in the same classes, played the same sports and hung out with the same friends. When we were younger, James had often gotten into trouble for the different pranks he would pull. When we started high school he got into the habit of undoing the bra of whatever girl sat in front of him. I would get into trouble just because I was his friend. Looking back, I feel sorry for James' parents and what they dealt with during those years. We were even brought to his home by the police once because of a fire that James had started. It was not a dangerous fire and no one got hurt, but the flames did burn down a park bench.

Even with the fire incident, James never got into a lot of trouble with authority figures because of his father. His dad was the wealthiest man in our hometown and he was friends with all of the 'influential' people: both Fire and Police chiefs, the Court bench, and even the Mayor. Because of that, James was never severely punished beyond a basic 'slap on the wrist' for the things he did, which were not really major offences to begin with. Nevertheless, his father was always hard on him and when James got into trouble, his father would look to me with disappointment apparent on his face. Once, James' father told me that he hoped my friendship with James would help keep him out of trouble and he knew that if James and I had not been friends, the pranks might have been a lot worse.

Even though James and I were best friends, we led different lives. He was from a wealthy background, while I had grown up in an average, middle class house. His father was always there pushing him to be more and to do more, while his mother was distant and always away visiting 'relatives'. In reality, I think she did not like being a mother; it made her feel old. She was never around anything that reminded her of her age, specifically James.

My parents were different. My mother was there for me when I needed her to be, but never unconditionally. There was a hidden wall that I was never able to get past. My father, on the other hand, was a typical father when I was a little boy until he discovered alcohol and things changed; he changed. When the war happened, he was conscripted and when he came back, he changed again. He did not touch alcohol after the war, nor did he touch my mother or anyone else for that matter. He formed this cocoon around himself and he did not let anyone in. After that, I spent more time with James and his father than I did my own.

James' dad was hard on him. He expected him to be the best of the best at everything and when James did not live up to his father's expectations, I knew he took it hard. My dad, as I said earlier, was barely involved with me. James and I were both on the track and field team, but whenever we had a meet or a race, my father never came to watch. James' father did and he cheered us on. I think James always resented me a bit because his dad acted as if I was his son as well; like I was the 'favourite'. But if James did resent me, he never said anything about it and when the race was finished, we would go back to our old selves.

We did everything together, so I was not surprised by the fact that when I was on the bus heading towards the town where the rail yard was, James was sitting beside me. At the time, I thought he was trying to prove something to his dad; that he was not useless. Regardless of what I thought though, I was glad for the company. Only later did I learn what James' actual reason for coming with me was.

There we were, in line for what was going to be the physically hardest time of our lives. After we registered, we went to find our cabins and it turned out that we had been placed in the same one, Cabin 3569.

The cabin was small. While other cabins were large enough to hold twenty men, ours was the runt of the litter; small and dilapidated even back then, so much so that I would be greatly surprised if it was still around today. The red paint on the window ledges was peeling off and the roof was a rusted green colour, which matched the adjoining outhouse. There was a porch from one side of the front of the cabin to the other, but it was only a foot deep and encased with something that was half way between chicken wire and mosquito netting. I think it was meant to keep bugs out, but it was not very effective seeing as one corner had collapsed in on itself.

The ground surrounding the cabin was the same as the rest of the yard and by the time we reached the door, my shoes were caked in mud. I took them off before we walked in. Once inside the cabin, we saw there were three other guys already present. Two of them were playing cards while the other one was sleeping. The two playing cards looked up when we opened the door and the smaller one got up and approached us. He was scrawny and did not look like he belonged working on a railroad. He had short brown hair, sunken brown eyes, and he sort of slithered over like he was trying to intimidate us. It did not work. I could hear James behind me snickering under his breath.

"Hi," he said.

"Hello," I responded in kind.

"What's yer name?" he asked.

"I'm Nathan and this is James. What's yours?" I asked him.

"Snake's the name, and the big guy back there's Al," he said pointing to the other card player.

It was all I could do to keep from laughing and I almost did until Al got up and came over. He was huge, at least six feet tall, built like an ox and he looked as though he could eat me for lunch and have room for seconds. His head was shaven and he had a tattoo of an anchor on his right arm.

"Think something's funny, do ya?" Al asked.

"No, not at all," I said. I elbowed James in the gut for him to be quiet.

"Good. The name's Al." At that, he stuck out his hand and when I shook it, he squeezed so hard I thought that he had broken mine. This caused Al to let out a roar of laughter. "Welcome to cabin 3569. I share a bunk with that guy over there," he said, pointing to the guy sleeping on the far bunk. "Don't mind him, he sleeps most the time 'cept when he's workin' and he usually keeps to himself then too. Snake has the top of this bunk and our other friend has the bottom of that one, so y'guys can fight over who gets what," he explained. "What shift's ya work?"

"I have afternoons and he has nights," I told him.

Al nodded towards James. "James, right?" James nodded. "Cool, yer with Snake, me, an' sleepin' beauty over there."

"What's his name?" James asked.

"Don't know, don't care. We start in a couple of hours so you'd better get unpacked," Al said as he and Snake went back to their card game. James grabbed the bunk with Snake, so I headed to the one that belonged to their other friend.

"Where's your friend?" I asked.

"Alex? Oh, he's working. He's got afternoons with you, so you'll meet him soon," Al answered without looking up from his cards.

When it was almost time for them to head off to work, the guy who was sleeping woke up. He got up, looked at James and I, grunted something and left.

"Told ya," Al remarked bluntly.

"Told us what?" I asked.

"I said he keeps to himself; most of the coloured folk do. I don't mind 'em too much. Most of 'em is real slow ya know, in the head, but they're good workers. Well, it's time we head out. C'mon kid, time to work," he said, grabbing James by the shoulder.

It had only been about fifteen minutes after they left when the door opened and a tall man with a medium build walked in, cursing something. When he saw me standing there, he paused for a moment, looked at me, then turned around and walked back outside. He was covered with mud and sweat and when he had looked at me, it was as if he had been studying me. I ignored it, thinking that he probably had the wrong cabin and I went back to unpacking my pack. When I was finished, I laid down on my bed to rest for a bit.

I woke up about half an hour later and when I sat up, standing in front of me was a naked man drying himself off. His back was to me so he did not see me. This was not the first time I had seen another guy naked, I was in sport teams at school after all, but for some reason this man had captivated my attention.

I lost myself in the sight of his body. My mind showed me his entire body from what was directly in front of me to what it created for the parts that were hidden. I followed the straight lines of his neck and his smooth back, to the curves of his buttocks. In my head, I could see what his abs looked like and the way his chest was scarcely decorated with hair that traced its way down to just above his pelvis. I could not help but stare as he pulled his pants on and turned around. When he saw me staring he immediately turned red in the face as I felt the heat rise in my own face. There was an awkward silence hanging in the air. I looked away and focused on one of the floorboards on the other side of the cabin. It was then that he first spoke to me.

"Sorry for waking you," he said.

"No, you didn't. I'm sorry. I didn't mean to stare," I said, briefly looking up at his face and quickly darting away again when we locked eyes.

"It's okay. I'm Alex," he said. His voice was smooth, just on the edge of being rough; a baritone voice that was both comforting and yet set me on edge. A voice that would make my heart skip a beat whenever I heard it.

"Nathan," I replied.

"Well Nathan, did you just arrive here?" he asked, heading towards his dresser. When I knew his back was turned towards me, my embarrassment eased and I was able to look up.

"Yeah, we just came in today," I told him.

"We?" he questioned.

"Me and James; a friend of mine from home," I explained.

"Oh, and where is this friend?" he asked.

"He's working already. He's on nights with Snake and Al I think their names were, oh and the coloured guy," I said.

"Jake," Alex stated bluntly.

"I'm sorry?" I asked.

"Jake. The 'coloured guy's' name is Jake," he told me, his voice taking on an almost sharp, warning edge to it.

"Oh, okay."

"Your friend, he is in our cabin then?" Alex inquired.

"He is," I replied.

"Well that's good," he said. "Do you work mornings?" he asked, coming over to the bunk we were to share.

"No I work afternoons," I told him, "with you."

"That's cool," he said smiling slightly as he stood there thinking about something. He was looking at me, but more staring into me then at me; seeing me in a way that made me feel both naked and alarmed at the same time. He had this glow emanating from him. The light made his tanned, smooth skin radiate. Our eyes were locked together and a million years could have passed between us, yet in the same instant, time seemed to stand still. I finally broke eye contact, my eyes falling to his mid-abdomen, slowly following the lines drawn like roads across his body. My hand ached to touch them.

He was the first to break the silence. "Listen, it's a nice night and I was about to go for a walk, do you want to come? I can show you around this place if you like."

"Thanks, that'd be great," I told him.

Alex nodded in agreement as he grabbed a loose plaid shirt and threw it on without buttoning it up. I put on my shoes, now dry and free of mud, and we left the cabin, heading out into the cool evening.

Chapter Two

Out in the yard, Alex showed me everything. First we went to the main office, which held a wall-sized corkboard. This was where we were supposed to go to find out where we were needed each day. Next he showed me where the showers were. We walked inside to murky white tiles that were yellowed with age and use. They covered the walls, floor and ceiling. Alex told me that the showers looked grungy now, but after a day's work getting covered in sweat and dirt, they would look like heaven on earth.

After we wandered around the compound for a bit he asked me if I was hungry – which I was – so we stopped off at the mess hall. The mess hall was a long half-cylindrical room. It was the kind you see in movies about World War Two that look like a farm silo cut in half. It had high ceilings with a door on one end and the kitchen on the opposite side. There were pairs of windows lined up on each wall facing each other, except in one spot where there was a hallway leading away from the main area to the washrooms. In the middle, stretching from one end to the other, there were twenty to thirty picnic tables, connected in thirds.

We both picked up supper and when I sat down, instead of sitting across from me like guys did at school, Alex sat right beside me. I could feel the warmth of his body and smell the sweet scent of his aftershave; the two consumed me.

"Aren't you going to eat?" he asked, looking over at me.

"Oh yeah, sorry, I was just thinking," I said, focusing on the food in front of me.

"About what?" he asked.

"Oh nothing, I was just wondering how James is doing," I lied.

"James? Oh right, your friend."

"Yeah, he isn't used to this sort of labour. Actually, he isn't used to any sort of labour, so it wouldn't surprise me if he quit tomorrow," I said, which made Alex laugh.

"So have you guys been friends long?" he asked.

"Since we were kids. We went to school together," I explained.

"That's cool."

"What about you three?" I asked. I managed to swallow a bite of mashed potatoes, which was closer to the taste of paper than anything else.

"Who?" he asked.

"You, Snake, and Al. You guys don't seem like you'd hang around each other. I mean they do, but not you," I said.

"Why not?" he questioned.

"I don't know. It's just that something seems fake with them, you know, like they're from one of those gangster films," I explained.

"But not me?" he asked, watching me from the corner of his eye.

"No, not you," I replied shyly.

"Why?" he asked. At this point I knew I was blushing and Alex could see it.

"Well, you don't seem fake. You're not trying to be something you're not, at least I think so. I'm sorry, I know they're your friends and I don't know them enough to say anything, so never mind," I said and he smiled.

"Don't worry about it. Everyone's entitled to their opinion, but you are right," he said. "I never really noticed but you're right, they do seem like they're from a gangster film." he laughed. "I know we don't look like we would hang around each other. I guess if it weren't for this place, we probably wouldn't. It's kinda funny, but they're fun. Don't let Al's size intimidate you; he just likes to play big, ya know what I mean?"

"Yeah, I do," I said.

"But yeah, we have a pretty good time," he said, eating a spoonful of paper potatoes.

A few guys came by and Alex introduced them to me. "We'll be working with these guys tomorrow. Nathan, meet Tom, Rick, Frank, and Larry. Guys, this is Nathan. He's bunking with Snake, Al, and me. He's on our shift." They all said hello to me and Frank gave me a slap on the back. After a few minutes of talking about which foreman to avoid and which to ignore, we were left alone again.

"Where are you from?" I asked Alex after eating a few more bites.

"Lakefield, it's the town just down the road from here. You?" he replied in question.

"About twenty miles north of Toronto, just a little town called Aurora," I said.

"Cool. So, you got a girl?" he asked, offhandedly.

"I'm sorry?" I asked.

"Do you have a girlfriend?" Alex repeated.

"Oh, no, do you?" I asked.

"No," he stated bluntly. I looked up at him as he was taller than me and the fierce look on his face told me not to press the matter. I turned back to my plate of food and began to eat slowly. "The food here isn't too bad, you'll get used to it," Alex said after a moment of awkward silence.

"It's okay," I mumbled, my mouth full of something someone tried to pass off as meatloaf. I thought I was eating sand.

"Do you like films?" he asked, changing the subject.

"Yeah, I like 'em. Is there a cinema nearby?" I asked, recovering from my mouthful of meatloaf.

"There's an outdoor one around the corner from here. I'll show you when we're done," he stated.

We soon finished up and headed out to where a large screen had been placed at the bottom of a hill. Along the hill, people had already grabbed spots to sit. There were a bunch of couples sitting together; guys and girls. Most of the guys had a girl with them, otherwise they sat in larger groups.

"They let us have visitors when we're not working," Alex explained. "Most guys bring their girlfriends," he said, his voice trailing off. I looked over to him and he was concentrating on something in front of him. He looked over at me, noticed that I was watching him, and smiled slightly. "Doesn't matter though, we can still sit and watch. It looks like they're playing some kinda romance flick tonight. Do you wanna stay and watch?"

"I wouldn't mind watching if you want to," I told him.

"Well, let's see how it is. We'll leave if it's too girly," he said.

"Okay, where d'you want to sit?" I asked. I hoped he would choose a spot where no one would notice me, the new guy, and the fact that I was with another guy, not a girl.

"At the top," he suggested.

Alex walked in front of me and chose a spot away from everyone else, at the base of a large oak tree. It was at the edge of a small forest, one of many that surrounded the compound. He took off his shirt and laid it down for him to sit on, but when he sat, he only took up half of the shirt. I was about to sit down on the grass when he told me that I had better sit on his shirt, so I would not get grass and mud on my pants. I was hesitant at first, but I eventually sat down. Once I was seated, he shuffled close to me, so again his warmth and smell consumed me.

I did not even notice when the movie started, nor did I care. I was too interested in this complete stranger who had captured me. As he sat there watching the movie, I was sitting there watching him; the outline of his face, his sharp chin, his deep blue eyes, and the way his hair naturally fell to one side of his head. I was entranced with his features. No, I was entranced with him.

He must have felt me watching him because his cheeks started to turn a light rose colour, so I quickly turned back to the movie. Some blonde was running into a man's arms crying, but again, I did not care. Alex shuffled closer to me so that his arm was touching mine and he was leaning against me. My heart started to pound so loud that I swear everyone could hear it.

"Is this okay?" he asked quietly.

"Is what?"

"What I'm doing. Is it okay?" he asked again, slightly leaning away from me.

"Yes," I said, equally quiet and I leaned toward him. He did not say anything as he relaxed himself against me, returning his attention to the movie. We sat there watching a movie that did not exist to me. All that existed was this man whom I had only met a couple of hours ago. All I could smell was him, all I could feel was him, all I could hear was him. His breathing soon melted with mine and we were like one body, breathing in and out, feeling the same thing.

About halfway through the movie, he got up saying that we should head back to the cabin and get some sleep because tomorrow would be a long day for me. I got up, picked up his shirt from the ground and we headed back toward our cabin, leaving behind the memory of us being as one; breathing as one and sharing our warmth.

Chapter Three

My first day of work was as physically hard as I thought it would be. It would have been a lot worse if Alex had not been there to guide me through it. We were assigned to a team responsible for laying down the wood that the iron beams of the rail lines were to be fastened to. Larry, Frank and Rick were on the same team as us. We were told to pair up into groups of two and Alex paired himself with me.

I could not figure him out. We barely knew each other. Hell, we had only known each other for ten hours, yet here we were, acting as if we had known each other our entire lives. He knew what I needed when I needed it, before I even asked. We had entire conversations without saying a single word.

Alex was a quiet man; quiet and intense. I learned a lot about him just from working with him. He was a hard worker and he barely rested. While other guys would talk about the girl they had just met, or the scores of whatever team had played the night before, Alex would focus on his work. Even with this tendency to be enveloped in his work, he was always aware of when someone needed his help or had questions about what needed to be done. He was clearly our foreman's 'go-to-guy' but he never let that go to his head. His nature would not let something like that cause his ego to swell.

It was clear he was well liked by the guys we were working with and they were friendly with me as well. Though I think they were friendly with me because Alex had decided to pay what attention he did not spend on his work, on me. Most of that attention was helping me to lift and check the placement of the different trusses, making sure the spaces were even and correct. I knew I would not have been able to do it without him.

A few times, whenever I was resting for a moment from all of the heavy lifting, I caught myself watching him. My eyes would trace along his arms and watch his shoulder muscles ripple with every board he lifted. I think it was the graceful way he lifted, lowered and moved about that first made me realize there was something different about him when compared to the other guys. They were just as good at lifting, moving and lowering the trusses as he was and some were better. They were able to lift heavier boards or lay them a little faster, but their movements were broken or awkward at times, whereas Alex was always graceful; with liquid-like movements.

I, on the other hand, was about as graceful as a blind man walking on a tight-rope. My muscles had never worked so hard in my life. I could feel them ripping and straining with every board I laid down and I felt my joints lock in place a few times. It seemed like all of my years readying myself for sports in high school was all for naught because I could not lay a wooden log on the ground without faltering. There were a few times I got extremely frustrated with my lack of ability to do the job. Whenever I was about to give up at what I was doing, Alex would walk over and tell me that it was okay, it was supposed to be hard, or he would simply grip my shoulder as he passed and I would to get my strength back.

During lunch break, I was so sore that if I stopped moving I knew my muscles would lock in place and I would not be able to do anything. When I said this to Alex, he laughed and told me to sit down. He sat behind me and began to massage my shoulders. It felt so good. My shoulders were aching and I welcomed his touch.

We sat together with his legs wrapped around mine. Even though we were hot and sweaty having him close to me, intimately close, sent a mixture of emotions flowing through my body; a combination of arousal and alarm. I suddenly felt extremely uncomfortable and exposed with Alex giving me a massage out in the open. After looking around to see if anyone was watching, I realized there were others doing the same thing. I started to relax and almost became lost in his touch. I say almost, because there was still a lingering alarm ringing in my head I was trying to block out.

After lunch was finished and we were back to work, I began to notice how dirty I was getting. My body was soaked in sweat and I had both dirt and soot smeared across my face as well as my hands and arms. The more I realized how dirty I had become, the more I started to dread going into the showers after work. I did not like the idea of being exposed to a room full of other men, least of all Alex. With what had happened to me when I saw Alex changing the previous day, I was afraid of what would happen if I was naked in the same room with him. As the time grew closer to ten at night, when our shift ended, my nerves began to fray and I developed a knot in the pit of my stomach

When the foreman called out that it was time to head back to the compound, I lost my voice. Alex walked with me and I could not bring myself to say anything to him. I had the feeling I was going to be sick if I said a single word. I looked over at him right before we reached the truck and he had a withdrawn look on his face. I recognized that face as the one from the man who had entered the cabin the previous day, now that it was covered in soot, sweat and mud.

Before we headed into the building that housed the showers and lockers, the foreman called out to Alex to speak with him. I took the opportunity to quickly change, so I would not have to face Alex's body. The locker room was not much of a room as it was just two long rows of lockers pushed to the side of the main shower area. The showers themselves were not private at all. There were shower heads enough for sixty men, with rows along the walls and posts scattered throughout the room, each post housing four heads. I did not like the idea of being exposed so I chose a shower head in one of the corners. That way, I could turn to face the wall if I became too nervous. As I headed towards the shower with a towel wrapped around my waist, I saw Alex walk into the locker room. We locked eyes for a brief moment before I turned away and made my way to the far corner of the room; putting as much distance between Alex and myself as possible.

I made a point of showering quickly, so I could get back to the cabin and dress as soon as possible. I showered with my back facing the room. Now that I knew Alex was in the room, I did not want to risk seeing him shower and become excited as I had before. After I washed my hair, I turned to the side to wash my back and I instantly locked eyes with Alex; he was showering at the post beside me.

My eyes found their way to just above his pelvic area before I could stop them. I felt heat start to gather between my legs, so I looked up to his face and saw that he was doing what I had; he was looking at my body. I was not prepared for something like that to happen. I felt sick to my stomach. I became shaky and felt slightly dizzy. I reached out for the wall to steady myself causing Alex to notice that something was wrong.

His face had a serious and alarmed look on it, but before he could ask any questions, I turned away from him and quickly finished showering. I did not look at him as I passed him on my way back to the lockers. By the time I gathered my things to head back to the cabin, I was on the verge of tears and feeling a mixture of sickness and sadness that I had not felt for years. I hurried back to the cabin and dressed quickly. By the time I was finished, Alex returned; his clothes in his hands and a towel around his waist.

"Are you okay?" Alex asked, apprehension lacing his voice.

"I'm fine," I lied.

"Listen, I'm sorry I made you feel uncomfortable, I didn't mean to," he said avoiding my eyes.

"It's okay," I said.

"No, it's not. I thought with what happened last night..." he trailed off.

"You thought right," I told him, taking a step closer. "It's just that I am not used to this sort of thing, you know? But that doesn't mean I don't like it or don't want it to happen."

We stood there watching each other. I could tell from the look on his face that he knew there was more to it than what I had said, but he did not press the matter which I was grateful for. He was locked in a pensive state.

"Come here," he said after a moment of silence.

"Why?" I asked, taking a small step backwards.

"Come here," he said again, his voice softening.

As I slowly came towards him, Alex dropped his clothes on the floor and closed the cabin door. When he turned back around, he let his towel fall to the floor which caused me to stop where I was. My body started shaking. He moved towards me and took me in his arms where he held me; his wet, naked body against my clothes.

I had a mixture of emotions whipping through my mind with this newfound intimacy. I was both excited and afraid. That alarm sound from the night before returned; slightly louder this time. I pushed it to the back of my mind where it belonged and turned my focus back to the fact that this man - this beautiful man - had his arms around me and was holding me close against his naked body.

His body was firm, not soft and smelled of spice, instead of a sour smell. He held me gently as if he were afraid that he might break me if he held any tighter. He held me close and I became lost in him. I began to feel at peace in his arms. I began to feel a safety with him that I knew was not false. I stopped shaking.

We were locked in each other's embrace for what seemed like hours, but was merely minutes before he backed up and looked me in the eyes. We did not speak until he broke away so he could get dressed. I sat on the edge of his bed, watching him as he performed the simple task of putting on clothes. The gracefulness of his movements was enchanting. In fact, there was very little about this man that I did not find mesmerizing.

"Come on," Alex said once he was dressed, "let's get some food." He paused. "You might want to change your clothes. Sorry, they're soaking wet now," he smiled slightly.

"They're fine," I smiled. "They'll dry soon."

At that, we left.

Chapter Four

The next day, things progressed in quite the same way as they had on my first day. We were assigned to the same task we had been assigned to the previous day. Alex and I paired together again and work passed in much the same way. My muscles were still sore from the previous day, so I was moving a little slower than I had been, but Alex told me that was to be expected. He also joked that if I thought my muscles were sore now, I should wait and see what they would be like the next day. I did not laugh, making him and Frank, who was sitting beside us at the time, laugh harder.

The day went on without any incident. At lunch time, we sat on a log to eat and Alex sat beside me. Once we finished eating, he told me to turn so he could massage my shoulders or else my arms would give up before we were finished. I agreed with him, so I turned my body. He shifted closer to me to get a better grip and I unconsciously leaned into him. Soon, I could feel him pressing hard against my lower back, causing heat to rise between my legs. I was lost in his touch again until one of the guys burst out laughing loud enough to jolt me back to where we were. I think it reminded Alex too, because he shifted away from me a bit and I leaned forward so we were no longer touching.

Alex stopped the massage soon after, telling me that he needed to speak to someone before lunch break was over. He left and I remained where I was, my heart thumping forcibly and my breath coming in short bursts. I knew then that I had to take care around him; I could not let myself lose my guard. I feared what might happen if I lost control, which was something I could never let happen.

When our shift was over and we were walking over to the truck that would bring us back to the compound, Alex leaned over and whispered in my ear to shower with him. I simply nodded my head because I could not speak. I had that same nauseous feeling from the day before, but this time it stemmed from fear of not being able to control myself. However, I knew because Alex wanted me to shower next to him that he would not let anything happen. At least, I hoped he would not.

I changed much more slowly this time. The previous day I had been in such a rush to avoid Alex that I had forgotten about the scars on my back and abdomen. They were not overly large, but they were noticeable; especially back then, when I was nineteen and they were fresher. I realized as I was changing that Alex was eventually going to see them and I knew he was going to ask questions. I wanted him to go into the showers first so he would not see me until we were surrounded by steam.

By the time I was finally undressed, Alex was already leaving the lockers. He headed into the shower area and turned his head to check if I was following him. I was. He moved back to the corner where we had showered the previous day and he took the same spot. I went to the one beside him and turned the hot water on. Through the steam, I could still see his body, but I had a hard time seeing any of the other guys, which meant they had a hard time seeing us.

Alex noticed me looking around and concern showed on his face, but I smiled at him to reassure him. I started to relax and I watched him shower without reservation. I looked up at his face and saw that he was also watching me. This time, the panic did not arrive as intensely as it had the day before. The thought of him seeing my body made me nervous, but I enjoyed having him watch me. I became aroused and my body reacted in turn. I covered myself but Alex shook his head no, so I turned to face the wall; that way Alex could see, but no one else could. He followed suit and I noticed that he was just as aroused as I was.

It was difficult to see him fully because of the steam, but what I could see intensified my arousal. He was beautiful and I had a desire to touch every inch of him. My desire surged to the point that I felt like I was going to explode. We soon finished showering and had to hide ourselves as we walked back to the lockers and grabbed our clothes. We wrapped our towels around our waists, I put my shirt on, and we used our clothes to cover the swelling under our towels.

As we approached the cabin, my heart was racing. I was not sure what was about to happen between us, but I knew *something* was going to. I walked in first and Alex came in after. He closed the door and I froze in place. He reached out, turned me around to face him, and let his towel drop to the floor. My eyes slowly traced their way down his firm body until they reached his pubic hair. His penis was large and thick, but proportionate to his body. I felt mine grow beneath my towel once again.

Alex slowly reached over and pulled my shirt off, which loosened my towel so it fell to the floor. I was now fully exposed to him and that raw nakedness caused me to shake. Even though I was nervous, I remained erect. He took a step closer; almost close enough to be touching. He was not looking at my body as I expected, instead he was watching my eyes. I trepidatiously reached up and traced the lines of his chest. He took my hand and pulled me into him so our bodies were fully touching each other. He wrapped his arms around me to stop me from shaking and I soon did.

He pulled me over to his bed and climbed in, motioning for me to follow. I was nervous again; afraid of what he was expecting from me. But when I lay down beside him, instead of touching me, he held his own cock and stroked it. After watching him for a minute, I followed his lead and stroked myself, with my eyes never leaving his hand. As I was getting close to climaxing, I looked up into Alex's eyes and he nodded before closing them. I watched as he leaned towards me and exploded onto my chest and stomach. Watching him caused me to fully climax and I shot all over myself and his body.

We lay there, side by side, breathing heavily until I started to laugh. He smiled and shifted onto his side so he was fully facing me. "What's so funny?" he asked.

"This. Us. What just happened. I've never came so much and so intensely before in my life. I didn't know I could. I blame you," I said, poking him in the stomach, making him laugh with me.

Alex got out of bed and threw my towel at me to clean myself as he did the same. We did not say much as we cleaned ourselves and then dressed. If he noticed the scars then, he did not mention them and I quickly forgot my worries. We walked over to the mess hall and ate in silence; only it was not an awkward silence as we both smiled the entire time. We had this secret moment between us that drew us together in a special and unique relationship. It was causing us both to radiate with life.

After supper, we walked outside into the cool night. I expected him to suggest watching the movie that was playing, but he breathed in deeply and said, "Let's go for a walk."

I agreed and we started walking. As I did not know the area, I followed Alex's lead. We walked in silence until we reached a lake just outside of the compound boundaries. He moved to the far edge of the water, at the boundary of a forest that surrounded the lake on one side, and sat down in the sand. I followed and sat beside him, looking out at the moon's reflection; sparkling like a gem in the waves.

After a few minutes of silence, Alex spoke. "There is something I think we need to talk about, something I've been thinking about for most of the day." My heart started to pound. I was nervous about what he was going to say. I shifted myself so I was facing him. When I did not respond, he continued. "We need to be very careful with how we act and what we do. When we are alone, we can relax, but when we are out in public, we have to be cautious. No one, and I mean no one, can know what we do. I mean it, absolutely no one," he said looking into my eyes. "Not even James."

"I know that," I finally said. "I know how people act towards fags."

"We're not fags and don't ever say we are again," Alex said sharply with anger in his voice.

"Okay, then what are we?" I asked, aware I could be causing a fight.

"I don't know," he said a bit more calmly, "but we're not fags." Silence followed this statement until I broke it.

"I'm sorry about today, at lunch. I didn't mean to forget where we were, but any time I'm close to you, close enough that we're touching, I get lost in your touch or in the warmth of your body and I have a hard time concentrating," I confessed.

"I know, the same thing happens to me, which means we have to be careful when we work. I don't think I should give you anymore massages. Do you think you'll be okay at work if I don't?"

"I'll have to be. You are right though, we shouldn't be that close while we're working. I was excited for the rest of the shift, which made me nervous."

"Okay, so while we're working and out in public, we can't be close to each other," Alex stated.

"But don't be too far from me. Now that we've gotten this close, I don't think I could handle you avoiding me," I said with a smile, even though I meant every word.

"I won't avoid you," Alex said, lightly moving his hand from my bicep to linger on top of my hand for a moment before sliding his hand in mine and holding it. I looked down at our joined hands and I knew in that moment there was something special about this man, something that had captured me. I shifted back so

I was leaning against his shoulder as we looked out onto the lake, our hands still intertwined.

"Can I ask you something?" he asked after a while.

"Of course."

"Have you ever done this with anyone before?" he asked hesitantly.

"Done what?" I asked, stalling for time.

He let go of my hand. "You know what I'm talking about, don't be stupid," he said, clearly annoyed.

"No I haven't," I told him, which was true, mostly.

"Don't lie to me."

"I'm not lying. You are the only one I have done this with. I've never even gotten this far with a girl," I confessed. He stared into my eyes, searching for the truth. He relaxed after looking into my eyes for a moment.

"Okay," he said. "Good."

I turned to face the lake again and he leaned against me, only I wasn't as relaxed as he was. I was worried, but I could not let him notice. I buried my anxiety and leaned into him. I was not sure what was going to happen between us, but I was not going to let my past ruin our future.

Chapter Five

Alex and I got into a comfortable routine. We would always try and work together, and then shower side by side. Depending on how much steam was present and how well we were shielded from the other guys influenced how close we got when we showered. Afterwards, we would head over to the mess hall to get something to eat, unless we became aroused during the shower. On those days, we would head back to the cabin and watch each other toss off. That was as far as we ever got. Beyond a hug or occasional caress, we rarely touched each other, not even when we were alone in the cabin. I do not know the reason, but I did not want to push Alex too far. I let things happen as he made them happen. I could tell by his moods that he needed to be in control of our situation, so I let him be.

Regardless of whether we simply changed or did more while in the cabin, we always went to the mess hall afterwards. Occasionally we were joined by other guys we worked with. Once we finished our food, we would either go for a walk or watch a bit of whatever movie was playing, depending on what Alex wanted to do. Every night they had a different movie. Whenever it was a western or a gangster film, we would sit with the other guys from work. For other movies, we would sit together at the base of our oak tree, leaning on each other.

Some days we would get up early and talk for a while and wait for James and the others to come back from their shifts. To my surprise, James actually enjoyed what he was doing. He and the guys were working in the metal shops, welding and preparing the iron beams that made up the tracks. He told me that, at first, the job was really tough, but now that he was used to it, he liked it.

Alex, Snake, and Al would carry on with each other while James and I would talk. After a few days, Alex began to involve me in what was going on with him and the guys. The first couple of times, Al gave us a strange look, but eventually he accepted the fact that James and I had joined their group.

Jake, on the other hand, had a tendency to keep to himself. Occasionally, Al would make a comment about him or call him names, but Jake would just ignore him. I always felt sorry for Jake. He was here on his own and, as far as I knew, he did not have any friends. Regardless of Al, Jake went on with his work and did what he needed to do.

We had one day off a week and on those days Alex and I, or James and I, would go wandering around in the fields surrounding the yard and town. Or the five of us would go swimming in the lake. At night, Al and Snake would head into town to go drinking and James always went with them. Alex and I would join them too on occasion, but not all of the time. I did not like going. I could not stand the smell of the place; the smell of urine, smoke, sweat and beer. It made me sick to my stomach. Sometimes Alex would drink with them. He knew that I was bothered by it, but he did not know why. On the first night he drank, when we were alone he tried to get close to me, but I could not do it. I could not bring myself to touch his skin when he smelled like whiskey and beer. I could tell by the look in his eyes that he wanted to ask me why, but he never did. He accepted the fact that when he decided to drink, I would not be near him.

Life went on like this for about a month until one day while we were watching a film, Alex turned to me.

"Are you happy?" he asked me.

"What do you mean?" I questioned.

"Are you happy with us?" he repeated.

"Of course I am," I replied. I was becoming anxious about where this line of questioning was leading to.

"Even though we have to keep things secret and can't be ourselves unless we're alone?"

"Yes. I know why it has to be a secret and I can deal with that. Why are you asking this? What's going on?" I asked, trying to figure out where he was coming from.

"Nothing," he half-mumbled.

"Come on, what?" I asked again.

"Do you like me?" he asked, shyly.

"Yes," I simply stated.

"How do you know that?"

"Because I've never felt this way about anyone before," I admitted both to him and to myself.

"Me neither," he confessed.

"So what's going on?" I asked.

"Nothing, I've just been thinking."

"About us?"

"Sort of. I'll tell you later, when we're alone," he said, which was all the invitation I needed. I stood up and he looked surprised.

"Well, let's go. Besides, the movie isn't that interesting," I stated with a smile. Before he could respond, I started down the hill and headed towards the cabin. He caught up with me and pushed me to the side. I laughed and pushed back. Before he could retaliate, I sprinted into a run and ran to the cabin, quickly reaching it before he did.

"Where'd you learn to run so fast?" he asked once he caught up with me.

"Track and field," I smiled. We quickly entered the cabin, turned on the lights and closed the door, an act that had become a habit of ours. I moved to his bed and sat down. "So, what's the big issue that has captured your attention?" I asked, as Alex came to stand in front of me.

"This." he leaned over and kissed me. I just sat there completely surprised, not knowing what to do. I mean, I have kissed before, but never like this. It had never meant anything in the past, but this time, it was something more, something I had never felt.

He straightened himself. "I'm sorry. I shouldn't have."

I did not let him continue talking. I stood up, leaned into him and touched my lips to his. He was surprised as I had never been the one to start anything between us, but that soon passed. We lost ourselves in each other; the feel of his lips on mine and the taste of his mouth. I thought I had been happy before, but this surpassed anything I had felt until now.

He moved away from my mouth and started to caress my neck with his tongue. His hot breath against my neck felt so good that I could feel the pleasure rush throughout my body. I was in heaven. I pulled him back and our lips connected again. He slipped his tongue into my mouth and I felt a new sense of pleasure. I returned the favour by moving down to his neck; tasting his flesh. It was a hot night so we were both sweating a bit and I could taste it on his neck; it was sweet. I moved up his neck, back to his face and up to his ears. When I reached his ear, he held me tightly and held his breath.

I could not stop, I was intoxicated with him. While I was teasing him with my mouth, he was holding me and moving his hands up and down my body. It felt so good. I returned to his lips and he lunged himself against me, kissing me passionately; even more so than he already had. I could feel his hard body against mine. I could feel his erection pressing against me. I was pushing him towards the door when he quickly spun us around and held me up against it. Our mouths connected.

He removed his shirt and slipped his hands under mine, so he could take it off. We held each other, our warm bodies radiating. I spun him around, his back against the door now, and brought our lips together again. I moved down to his neck, but instead of stopping there, I kept going. My tongue moved down his chest, across his abdomen and continued on its journey until I reached the top of his pants. I knew what he wanted me to do and, for the first time, I wanted it as well. This felt so perfect.

I unbuttoned his jeans and slipped them down past his thighs to the ground. His boxers soon followed. I opened my mouth and slipped his hard penis inside. The entire time I was there, he held me close to his body. I kept going until he climaxed into my mouth. After I wiped my lips, he was still shaking and pulled me up to trace the outline of my face with his fingers. I led him to his bed where we laid down in each other's arms. We laid there, immersed in each other.

I stayed with him until he fell asleep. I watched him sleep while I stroked his hair. The sun eventually began to rise which meant the guys would be back soon. I quietly slipped out from underneath Alex's arms, gathered the clothes we had left at the foot of the door, and climbed up into my own bed to fall asleep.

Chapter Six

The next day, my fears quickly turned into reality. When I woke that morning, I was in a fantastic mood. The previous night was fresh in my mind and I was excited to see Alex. The other guys had not come back from their shift yet, so I decided to give Alex a little surprise, but he was not there. His bed had already been made. The alarm in the back of my mind started to sound as a warning that something was wrong, but I refused to listen to it.

He could just be using the washroom, I told myself and headed over to the showers to find out. On my way, I ran into James heading toward the cabin, soaking wet and wearing a towel.

"Hi," I said in passing.

"Whoa, where are you off to in such a hurry that you can't talk to me first?" he called after me, causing me to stop.

"Nothing special, I just have to piss like a horse," I lied. "You haven't seen Alex by chance?" I tried to ask casually.

"Yeah, I saw him heading out before I took my shower, why?"

"Oh, no reason. I forgot to pack my alarm and he's been waking me up in the mornings, but he must have forgot." The siren in my head grew louder. "Anyways," I continued, "gotta run. I'll see you later!"

I headed towards the showers, even though I knew he was not there. After I verified my suspicions, I wasted time in the mess hall until it was time to start work, then I took my time walking over to the waiting truck. Three guys were already in the back, waiting for the rest of us to arrive. One of them was Alex.

I hesitated a bit before climbing in and it only took one look at his face to know that he did not want to talk to me. Instead of sitting where I usually did, near him, I sat as far from him as the truck bed would allow. When we arrived at the rail site, he looked at me and motioned with his head to tell me that I had to partner with him. This simple notion confused me. I assumed he did not want to see me since he left me alone earlier, so rather than moving, I just stood still, half-looking at him and half-listening to the warning in my head. It was not until Frank came up behind me, slapped me on the back, and made a joke about sleep-walking, that I actually moved.

The day progressed much the same way as it usually did. I worked on auto, letting my muscles perform the job they were used to doing. Alex focused on his work as usual, only he made a point to not look at me unless the job required it, which it rarely did. I let my mind wander to a different place, far from where we were; a trick I had learned a long time ago. At lunch, I wandered to the edge of the clearing the guys had designated as our break area and sat on the ground with my back facing everyone. Alex may have decided that he and I were going to work together, but that did not mean we had to eat together. I sat there, lost in thought, until I felt the hairs on my neck rise. I could feel a pair of eyes on my back, so I turned to confront them. On the opposite side of the break area sat Alex, his eyes focused so intently on me that he barely noticed I was looking at him. Once he did, he looked away, stood up and walked off. I turned around and returned to my barely touched food. We soon returned to work and finished the shift in the same manner we had started it, in silence.

Once the truck had returned us to the compound, I hopped off and slowly made my way to the showers. I quickly glanced to see if Alex was following. He was talking to the foreman about something, so I took this opportunity to avoid him. I changed quickly, washed at the closest shower head I could find and rushed to get clean. I showered in record time and finished before some of the other guys even started. As I left for the cabin, I briefly locked eyes with Alex heading into the showers. I broke contact with him and quickened my pace.

By the time I had finished dressing, it was still light out. I decided to spend the remainder of the daylight at the lake alone. Walking to the lake, I made a conscious effort not to look towards the showers so I did not accidently catch sight of him. I could not stand to see the avoidance across his face again. Having seen it for the entire day was enough.

The sun had just started to set when I sat down along the water's edge; my feet resting in the sand, being caressed by the calm surf. The sky was a rich blue with orange on the horizon. Across the lake, the other shore was made of rocks and pebbles rising into a small mountain. Two thirds of the way up, a tree line formed sporadically at first, then growing denser until turning into a forest that encased the top. The sun was setting behind the mountain, casting the mountain in shadow, turning it a deep royal purple. The setting was peaceful and I started to relax. The sky slowly filled with rich colours: peaches, pinks and light blues. The colours blending together with each one rich and vibrant, smudging into its neighbour, was beautiful. The golden sun started to fade and with it followed the peach, bleeding into a rich pink, then a deep red, where it ended as purple, leaving the top of the mountain lost in the richness of the night sky.

"When I was on day shift, I always loved watching the sunset from here." I quickly turned around to find Alex standing behind me, close to me, but still somewhat at a distance. "May I join you?" he asked. The formality in his voice made my stomach turn. He sounded as if this was the first time he had ever spoken to me.

"You may," I matched his formal tone.. I shifted in the sand to make a spot for him. He hesitated, looking as if he wanted to say something but instead he sat.

"Why didn't you shower with me?" he asked quietly. I looked over at him and tried to read his expression, but it was masked in shadow.

"I was afraid," I said, looking to my feet in the surf. There was silence between us, deafening silence.

"Afraid of what?" he asked hesitantly.

"You."

"Why?" he asked, surprise in his voice.

"Because you were avoiding me," I stated. I refused to look at him. I focused my attention on the reflection of the stars in the sky, now showing on the lake's surface.

"I wasn't avoiding you," he tried to argue.

"Yes, you were," I said flatly, which was followed by more silence.

"Why did you lie to me?" he asked.

"What are you talking about?" I asked, even though I had a feeling I knew the answer.

"The first time we sat here, I asked you if you had ever been with a guy and you said no. You lied," he said with anger tracing the edge of his voice.

"No, I didn't."

"Bullshit, Nathan. Last night you gave me a blowjob. How the hell did you know how to do that if you have never done it before?" he accused me. I finally looked over at him.

"I'm not ten years old, Alex. I've looked at adult magazines, I've seen what the girls do to the guys in those magazines, so I thought I would try to do the same to you. It doesn't take a university degree to figure out how to do it," I said, rather monotone in voice.

I did not want him to hear the emotions I was feeling; the distress that had risen with his accusatory question. He looked away from me, so I stared back at the lake. My heart was falling apart. He was going to end things between us, I knew it. The pain that was filling my body because of that thought was too much to bear. I needed to leave. Before I had the chance to stand up, Alex turned my head and brought his lips to mine. I could not control my emotions any longer. Tears started to fall from my eyes, so I pulled back. I quickly wiped them away, but not before he noticed their presence.

"Why are you crying?" he asked with trepidation.

"Because I don't know what to think or how to feel about you. This is new to me and I'm afraid of the feelings that have been growing in me. I was finally starting to get used to them and then today happened. It felt like those feelings were being ripped apart all day and I thought we, whatever we are, were over and now you are kissing me. I just don't know anymore." I began crying again and Alex reached up to wipe away the new tears that had started to fall. "God, look at me," I said wiping my face, "I'm sobbing like some stupid fag."

"Maybe," Alex said, lightly punching me in the arm, "but you're mine and that's what matters."

After a few minutes I stopped crying and started to feel like my normal self again. We stood up to head to the mess hall for dinner and as we were walking, he turned to me. "Don't hate me, but I need to hear it. Do you swear that you have never been with a guy before?" he repeated.

I turned to face the man I had fallen in love with, looked him straight in the eyes and lied. "I swear I have never been with a guy before you."

Chapter Seven

On one of the Sundays we had off work, Alex left the night before to go into town to visit his parents and would not be back until just before our shift started on Monday morning. Snake and Al had been saving up some of their money so they could rent a hotel room for the day, at one of those hotels where each room had a girl available to entertain the men that stayed there. That left James and I alone in the cabin, which I was pleased to discover. I was not upset with Alex or anything of the sort; I would have loved to spend the day with just him, but I had not spent much time alone with James, so I welcomed the opportunity. When we awoke Sunday, it was a beautifully warm morning, so we decided to go for an early swim. We headed to the showers to grab a pair of towels before heading to the lake. The sky was clear and there was barely a breeze in the air; a perfect day for swimming.

Being with Alex all of this time without him remarking or asking questions about my scars made me realize I had nothing to be ashamed of. I decided to prove that to myself by stripping nude and jumping into the lake. This would be the first time James had ever seen me nude. All of those times in school, after track and field practice or gym class, I had always skipped the showers because I did not want the other guys to see the scars and marks on my body. They were fresher back then, and therefore more visible. Once, I decided to take a shower after a particularly muddy outdoor gym class. James was not there that day, so he did not see, but the other guys in class did. After the shower, no one would look at me nor speak to me. It took them a few weeks to forget what they had seen and for things to return to normal. I decided then that I would never take a shower at school again.

When I came up for air I saw James was standing there looking at me in disbelief while holding onto his towel. I realized I had surprised him more than I thought I would have. I laughed and yelled out to him, "Are you coming in or not?" He laughed in response and decided to join me, removing his own clothes.

This was the first time I had seen James nude as well. He was fit, with a lean muscle structure, much different than Alex's more muscular body. His skin was fair in colour and as smooth as ivory. I realized watching him change that he was also very attractive; a fact that I had never bothered to register in my mind before. This new knowledge caused me to be aware of where I was looking as I tried not to stare at his body.

After swimming for a while, I got out of the water to lie down on my towel and dry off. Five minutes later, James came up from the water, threw his towel beside mine and joined me. As we were letting the sun dry us, he turned to me. "How come you never showered with the rest of us at school?"

James must have been thinking the same thing as I had been when I first jumped into the lake. I was a bit startled by the bluntness of the question, but I was not surprised he had asked it. I propped myself up so I could look over at him and saw his eyes tracing along my body, noticing the scars that have long since faded.

"No reason," I replied, still watching his eyes. "I guess I was just more self-conscious of my body back then."

He looked up and realized that I was watching him look at my body. He turned red in the face, looked away and turned his body so his stomach was against the towel. I got up and put my clothes back on saying, "Come on, I'm starving. Let's grab some breakfast."

James got up and put his clothes on, keeping his back to me the entire time he dressed. He remained silent as we dropped our towels off to be cleaned and headed to the mess hall for food. Once we started eating, whatever had been on his mind since the lake had disappeared and he started talking. We did not talk about anything of any consequence, just the usual small talk over eggs and bacon. After breakfast, I suggested we go for a walk. We headed out of the compound, onto the main road into town and over to a field by the highway. We laid there, gazing at the clouds that had formed since our swim, watching them move lazily along the sky.

"Do you miss home?" I asked, breaking the silence that had started when we entered the field.

"No," he replied, without hesitation.

"Not even your dad?" I asked, sitting up on my elbows.

"No. Do you miss yours?" he asked mockingly.

"Point taken," I said. "I don't know, I miss some of the people back home, but not everyone," I said, lying back down.

"What do you think is going to happen after we leave here?" he asked after more silence.

"I don't know," I confessed. I had no idea what to expect. I did not know what I was going to do when I finished working at the compound. And now that I had started to think about it, I began to wonder about Alex. I had developed strong feelings for him and I did not want to lose him. I was not sure what he wanted.

"What do you want to do after we're done here?" I asked James.

"I don't know. Maybe find a job at a mill or a steel yard somewhere I guess."

"What do you think your father will do?" I asked.

"I don't care what he does. He can jump off a bridge for all I care," he said, his voice laced in bitterness.

"I doubt he will be too happy about his son 'working like a commoner.' He probably has big plans for you to take over his business," I told him, matching his mocking tone.

"Probably. Don't mean I'm going to do it. I'll do what I want with my life," he said proudly.

"He must have freaked out when you told him that you were coming here to work."

"Oh hell yeah," he laughed. "He didn't see no reason why his son should be working like some bum off the streets," he said, mimicking his father's inflictions.

"Tell your dad I said thanks," I laughed, lightening the mood. It was getting too heated for my tastes.

"Oh I'm sure he'd make an exception for you. After all, you're like a son to him too," James said in a joking manner.

"Don't start on that," I nagged. "I'm just his son's only friend and he treats me good so you won't be a loner." I playfully punched his shoulder. "'Sides, he pays me on the side to be your friend." I laughed out, making him punch me back, hard. "I think I'll ask for insurance next time I see him," I said, holding my shoulder. "It's dangerous being your friend."

"I think I'll ask for a refund. You're a lousy friend," he joked, rubbing his hand. "And you're too bony."

Him saying that just made me laugh more. It was nice being able to relax with James and laugh. We spent pretty much the rest of the day lounging around in the field, joking with each other and play fighting like we used to do before I had decided to head into the world. It was a good day and I was happy.

We returned to the cabin when the sun started to set and quickly found out that spending all that time in the sun had given James a vibrant sunburn. Not long after James and I had returned to the cabin, Al and Snake came back to regale us with tales of sleazy girls and to see if James wanted to head into town with them to go drinking. They asked me to join them, but I said I was too tired and I was going to head to bed early. I really did not like the bars and the smell of alcohol. I was willing to endure it for Alex, but not without him.

They left me alone with my thoughts of the great day that had just transpired. I soon drifted off to sleep. I was woken up by Alex kissing me on the forehead.

"You're back early," I said, half asleep.

"Yeah, I had enough of my father's disapproving looks, so I thought I'd come back and surprise you," he said, leaning towards me.

"You're welcome to surprise me any day," I said, embracing him and bringing our lips together.

We stayed up for a while and he told me about his family. He had two older sisters that were both married with children. His father used this as an excuse to tell Alex he was wasting his life and that he needed to find a good girl and settle down. Alex and his father did not get along well, which I was starting to think was a theme with our generation.

Two hours later, the guys came back from the bar. Alex and I joined in their talk about the girls at the bar that night and how James had 'a real looker' hit on him, but he was too drunk to do anything about it. James was already passed out cold. After some time, we all drifted off to bed with a reminder that Alex and I had to work the next day.

Chapter Eight

The next evening, our foreman asked Alex to stay behind to have a meeting with him to discuss new procedures. Rather than waiting around for his meeting to finish, I went to the showers without him. I hoped the meeting would not take too much time. By the time I had fully showered - and taken my time doing so - Alex had yet to enter the showers, so I finished and made my way to the cabin. When I arrived, I was surprised to find Jake there and I startled him as well. He was sitting in a chair by the table, reading. When he saw me, he quickly hid the book underneath the table and put on a blank expression.

"What were you reading?" I asked him.

"Nothing," he mumbled. He kept his gaze on the table.

"I didn't know you could read," I said. As soon as the words left my mouth, I realized how they sounded and I regretted them immediately.

"Just 'cause I'm coloured, don't mean I can't read," he snapped back at me.

"I didn't mean it like that. Most of the guys here don't know how to read, black or white. Sorry, I didn't mean to offend you."

Jake continued to sit there, so I went to lie down on Alex's bunk to wait for him. After a moment, Jake pulled the book out from under the table and continued reading. "Do you have any friends here?" I asked.

"What's it to you?" he asked, clearly suspicious of me.

"I was just curious. I've never seen you with anyone," I plainly stated. I was not trying to tease him, I just never had the chance to speak with him before and I was not going to let it pass by. Ever since I had moved into the cabin, I had been curious about Jake. Not because he was black; that did not matter to me. I was curious because he did not fit in with Al and Snake, or some of the other guys at the compound. I guess I sympathized with him, for not quite fitting in.

"I don't need any friends," he remarked.

"Everyone needs friends," I replied.

"Well I don't," he was becoming defensive.

"What about your family?" I persisted. I was determined to find out something about this man, aside from the fact that he typically slept all day and liked to read in secret.

"Why you askin' me all these questions? You going to go an' tell the big guy so he can make fun of me some more?" he asked, looking up from his book. There was an anger radiating from his eyes that surprised me. I was not afraid of him, but in that moment, I could see that there was a passion in him and if it were released by the wrong person, Jake could become dangerous.

"No. I'm sorry he's cruel to you. I think it's rude and immature, actually." There was silence from him, so I laid back down on the bed. I heard him turn a page in his book.

"Yes I have family; my mother and two sisters," he said quietly after a few minutes of silence.

"What about your father?" I questioned.

"He's in Heaven. He died two years ago, which is why I'm here," he said.

"I'm sorry to hear that," I replied.

"You got a family?" he asked.

"Yeah, my mom and dad," I stated.

"Do you miss them?" he asked.

"I miss my mom."

"Not your dad?" Jake asked curiously.

"No," I stated flatly.

"Why?" he asked. I paused to think about what I was going to say.

"We don't get along," I decided to say. He did not reply. "Do you miss your family?" I asked, turning the conversation away from me and back to him.

"Every moment I'm awake, but they don't have nobody to take care of them now and my sisters need someone to look out for them," he replied.

"I don't think I'd be able to do that, have that much responsibility. At least not right now, I'm too young for that." I said. Jake started to laugh.

"You're never too young," he said.

"Well, how old are you?" I asked him, trying to prove my point.

"How old do you think I am?"

"I don't know… Thirty?" That made Jake laugh even harder.

"I'm only twenty-one," he said with a smirk.

I did not believe him at first. There was no way he was that young and I told him so. He took out his employee card, which had his date of birth on it, and proved me wrong. He was only two years older than me. Two years and he already had a family to support. This knowledge created a great deal of respect for him in me. After giving his card back, I sat back down on Alex's bunk.

"So, what book are you reading?" I asked again.

"Moby Dick."

"I hated that book. We had to read it in school and I just couldn't get into it. Do you like it?"

"It's not my favourite, but it's better than nothing," he said.

"What is your favourite book?" I questioned, curious of what his answer would be.

"Oliver Twist," he said with a smile.

"I can't believe this. Why aren't you like this around the others?" I asked, sitting up to face him.

"They leave me alone if they think I'm a dumb, black cotton-picker," he said with disgust.

"That's horrible," I replied.

"I suppose it doesn't bother me any. I like being left alone," he said, looking at me.

"Sorry." I smiled.

Alex walked in the cabin from his shower a few minutes later.

"Sorry I took so long. Hey Jake," Alex said. He looked at me. "Aren't you ready yet?" I realized that I was still in my towel. I got up and grabbed some clothes.

"I am now," I stated. As we left the cabin, I turned to Jake.

"Don't worry, your secret's safe with me." He nodded his head and went back to his reading.

Alex looked at me with a puzzled look. "What was that about?" he asked me.

"Nothing, come on I'm starving," I said as I started walking to the mess hall.

"Hey, wait up!" Alex called out to me.

Chapter Nine

The next few weeks passed without much incident. Alex and I were still working together but we made a conscious effort to not be too close to each other, lest someone should suspect something. We still showered together and on the days we became aroused over one another - which was happening more frequently - we returned to the cabin to watch each other pleasure ourselves or I would take him in my mouth.

After the first time I had him in my mouth, he was hesitant to be physical with me. However, that soon went away and he accepted my story of just copying the magazines. He enjoyed my tongue over just tossing off side by side, so I was asked to perform more frequently. He never once had me in his mouth. It was always me who did the work. I did not mind though, I was just happy to be with him and to make him happy. As I said, I knew not to rush things and to take them at his pace; to let him choose what happened and when.

On a Wednesday at the end of July, the foreman called all of us over to make an announcement. The lumber yard that provided us with the logs used for the ties laid for the rails had a major accident, causing our next shipment to be delayed. They would not receive the next shipment until the following Monday, therefore we were instructed to finish laying the pieces we had, and then the rail yard would be shutting down until Monday. People were welcome to stay in the compound as the mess hall, showers and outdoor movies would continue to run, but they were also free to leave. If they did not return on Monday for their shifts, they would no longer be employed and would not receive their last pay.

Everyone was excited and happy to hear this news since the weather had been beautiful these past few days and the weekend promised to be the same. We went back to work for the rest of the shift and again the next day, only to run out of lumber mid-shift. The guys on our shift celebrated this early night of freedom by heading out to the bar in Lakefield for some food and drinks. Alex and I went with them and we enjoyed ourselves.

We returned to find Al, Snake and James heading into town for a beer. We told them we had just returned from there, passing on their invitation to join them. That night, the compound had emptied out so much that it quickly became like a ghost town. Alex and I decided to make the most of the empty place. I suggested that we go for a swim in the lake in the moonlight. Alex was a little hesitant, but knowing the compound was empty, he soon warmed up to the idea.

After our moonlit swim, Alex told me there was something he wanted to show me, but it had to wait until tomorrow. I bugged him to tell me what it was, yet he refused to give me any hints.

He only said that we had to leave early to see it. We returned to the cabin, finding Jake asleep. He had not gone out with anyone. We went to bed soon after coming back and were sleeping long before the others came back from the bar.

The next morning, I was woken up by Alex whispering in my ear. I did not move, until he kissed me, then he knew I was awake. When he broke away, I was grinning and he returned my smile with his own.

"Good morning," I said, sleep still in my voice.

"Come on, get up. The sun's going to rise soon," he whispered to me as he climbed off of my bed to get ready.

When I rose, I noticed that the guys were still sleeping in their beds. I was surprised Alex risked kissing me in front of them, sleeping or not. I was not complaining however. I would start each day in the same fantastic mood if I were woken the same way every morning. We were determined to dress quickly and quietly so as to not wake the others. Let me tell you, trying to dress while not making a noise in a log cabin, where every single floorboard squeaks, is not easy. However, we were successful and, once dressed, Alex grabbed a blanket and we started walking towards the lake. The morning air was cool and crisp and there was freshly fallen dew covering everything. The air had an energy to it that we both felt and enjoyed.

We arrived at the lake just in time to catch the first rays of light appearing over the water. Alex quickly laid out the blanket on the shore so we could sit. We were sitting on the blanket with my head resting in his lap. We remained like that for a while, watching the sun stretch out before the sky with Alex absently running his fingers through my hair. Once the sun finished rising and the air began to warm, Alex got up and took off his shirt. I sat there watching him, following the lines of his muscles with my eyes. He saw me watching him and smiled. He came over to the blanket, pulled me up to my feet and we kissed.

"Come on, we should get moving so I can show you what I want to show you," he said.

"And what would that be?" I asked again.

"It's a surprise, follow me." He paused. "You might want to take your shirt off though; it's going to get hot."

"I'll be okay," I said, bending down to grab the blanket.

"Leave it there. We'll be back for it later," he said, walking away from me. We headed towards the woods on the far side of the lake; he was in front and I was closely following. As we were heading into the woods, it did become hot and the humidity increased, making the air heavy. I stopped to remove my shirt as Alex had suggested. He turned, saw what I was doing and laughed. "I told you it'd be hot," he smirked.

"Yeah I know. So, what's this big surprise?" I asked mockingly.

"You'll see. You're going to love it," he claimed, continuing to move forward.

"Not if it's in these woods," I said, brushing a twig from my hair. He just laughed. We continued walking towards our unknown destination, unknown to me that is. The further into the woods we walked, the more dense the trees became. We happened upon a creek bed that was lined with loose stones and jagged rocks. There was moss growing all around the base of the trees by the creek and on all of the rock surfaces. Alex took a running start and jumped over the water, landing with ease on the other side. I was not so graceful. I took the same running leap, but the rock I landed on was covered in slippery moss. I would have landed on my face had Alex not been ready to catch me and keep me from falling in. Once I steadied myself, we continued on our way.

I had a hard time keeping up with him. The trees became very closely knit, creating a canopy that allowed in very sparse patches of light. All around the trunks of the trees were many types of bushes and weeds that were so dense I could not see where I was stepping. As a result, I stepped into a gopher hole, getting my foot stuck. When I finally wiggled my foot free, I glanced up and realized I had lost sight of Alex. I started to call out his name. "Alex? Alex!"

"I'm here," he called back.

"Where?" I asked. "I can't see you."

"Just keep moving forward. Follow my voice," he said calmly. About three feet later, I broke through the trees and nearly fell into him. He was waiting there, smiling. "Ready?" he asked.

"Ready for what?" I asked.

"Your surprise."

"After those woods, it had better be good," I grumbled.

"It is." He pulled me into an embrace and brought his lips down to mine. I mildly resisted, but soon became enveloped in his smell and taste. After a moment, I pulled away and gave him a questioning look. He was standing there with a big grin on his face. "Surprise."

"That was my big surprise?" I asked, obviously annoyed.

"No, I just took advantage of the situation," he grinned.

"Cute." I said, stepping back and he laughed. "So, where is it?" I asked.

"There," he pointed. He moved to the side so I could see a set of iron gates behind him, across the clearing.

"Where do they lead?" I asked.

"You'll see," he said. He took my hand and led me across the clearing.

Chapter Ten

The gates were attached to large brick pillars, however one gate was only attached by the bottom hinge; the top hinge had rusted and broken off. Both were covered in ivy and were damaged by years of weather and lack of care. As we approached the gates, I noticed the remains of a wall. Most of the brick had fallen off, but the foundation was still there as well as a few scattered sections, though most were overgrown with ivy and grass. The gates had something written across them, but because of decay, it was hard to make out. The most I could get were the words "Gates Way." The rest was illegible. On the ground between the gates there were stones scattered all around. At first I thought they were pieces that had fallen off the wall, but as I got closer I realized they formed a shape like a river. It was a road that had broken apart over the years.

"What is this place?" I asked in wonder.

"You'll see," he said, continuing forward.

As we moved along the path from long ago, I smiled at him. I loved the feel of his hands; large and strong. The hands of a man. Even though they were strong, at the same time they were soft and gentle and I did not fear them. We moved along the path, passing a large oak tree where the branches stooped so low to the ground that we had to brush them aside to move past them. Through the leaves, I saw our intended destination which I fell in love with the moment I cleared the tree. Before me was an old and decaying cemetery. The road we were on led up to another stone wall, only this one was only as high as a child's waist. At the center was a picket gate that had rusted closed, forcing Alex and I to climb over a section of the wall to get inside. I could tell the gravestones were old, from the turn of the century, because they were not like those found today. They did not have pictures of loved ones, nor were they made out of illustrious rock such as granite and marble. No, these were from another time where they were made out of simple stone and only had the names, dates, and a small saying, if you were lucky enough to afford such a thing.

Most of the names and dates had all but worn away and all of the stones had stains and water marks on them, causing decolourization on the surfaces. There were a few however, where there was still some lettering, enough to make out a name or a date. I let go of Alex's hand to explore these monuments. A few were warm to the touch due to the scattered sunlight that broke through the tree tops covering the yard, protecting those that laid here.

"How did you know about this place?" I asked.

"I found it when I was a kid. One summer, I decided it was my mission to explore these woods and I found the wall surrounding this place," he explained.

I walked up to each one of the grave markers, running my hands along the top of them, feeling the smooth, worn stone. I continued along the way, trying to read the names until I came to one in particular. It was far in the back where the more grandiose gravestones were; the rich ones. It was tall like an obelisk, only it was of an angel. And, not one of those short Botticelli cherubs, this was an adult angel, carrying a sword as though she was guarding something or someone. I knelt down to the ground to read the name on it. Unlike most of them, the inscription on this one was clear and not worn away. It read, *"Shawn Patrick Gatesway."* That was the name on the gate in the clearing, Gatesway, not "Gates Way". He was, *"Born October 16th, 1874. Died October 16th, 1893."* He had been my age when he died. *"May you find the peace you longed for here and may this Angel guard your soul from harm for we were unable to guard you."* Reading the inscription nearly made me cry and I felt a pain in my heart. Whoever had this inscription made must have felt responsible for his death.

"A man tried to rob him and his parents while they were out for his birthday dinner. When his parents refused to give up the gold watch they had just bought for Shawn, the robber shot him so they wouldn't have any use for it," Alex explained when he came up behind me.

"That's horrible. How do you know?" I asked him.

"When I found this place, I asked my grandfather, who had been around at the time and he told me what he remembered from the papers. He also told me that the town had the monument created and renamed this place, Gatesway Memorial, in honour of Shawn. My Granddad also said that three weeks after the shooting, they found and hung the man who shot Shawn," Alex explained. "When I was older, I found some old records that confirmed a bit of what my Granddad had told me."

"Good, the bastard got what he deserved," I said with solid conviction in my voice. I felt a connection to this unknown person, this kid whose life had been stolen from him.

We must have stayed in that graveyard for at least two hours, wandering around and reading all of the stones. Alex told me what he had found out about certain ones: a mother who had drowned and an elderly couple who died in their sleep together. Each stone had a story. He also told me stories he had made up for the stones that he could not find any information about. There was one stone with a boy named John on it; he died when he was twelve. When I asked Alex about it, he said that it was a very sad story.

"I had a hard time finding out about this one; no one wanted to talk about it. What I did manage to find out was that he was abused as a child by his father. He wasn't just beaten, his dad would touch him and do things with him that you don't do to your kid. When his mom found out, she tried to stop him, but he in turn would hit her. People knew about the beatings, but they just ignored it. Beating your kid was normal. They just figured that John was a bad kid, so he must have deserved it."

"No one deserves that. No one," I stated, with anger in my voice.

"John couldn't stand it any longer so he wrote a letter about what was happening, the abusing and other things, and then he shot himself with his dad's gun."

"Did his dad get killed too? Like did they throw him in jail?" I asked, a strong need for vengeance behind my voice.

"Why would he? As far as anyone was concerned, a bad kid killed himself and the parents are the victims," Alex said with disgust. "No one believed the letter John had written about his father and nothing was ever done."

While hearing the story about John, I could feel a tearing happening inside of me. Memories came back to me and I tried to push them away. I could not let them come back. I was staring at the grave and I started to cry. Alex must have seen my tears because he came over to me and held me close to him, which just made me cry all the more.

When he asked me what was wrong, I could not tell him. I could not have him look at me as others have. So I told him I thought the story was sad and that was all.

"Come on, let's go. They will have started breakfast by now," he said.

"Okay."

"I'm sorry," he said.

"For what?" I asked.

"For bringing you here, I hoped you would have liked it," he confessed.

"I did! Believe me, I do. I love all of the history here." I kissed him. "It's just that John's story is a sad one, that's all," I explained.

"Okay, I'm glad you liked it," he replied.

When we passed back through the gates and started walking through the clearing, I did not say good-bye to those resting behind me. I knew I would be back here again.

Chapter Eleven

When we reached the mess hall, Snake, Al and James were there, getting their breakfasts. Once we sat down with them, Alex and Al started carrying on with each other. I looked over at James, but he would not look at me. He had barely touched his food. Al had asked him what was wrong and he told him that he was not 'feelin' right,' and then he looked at me. He was studying me, but

I did not know why. All throughout breakfast he kept on giving me odd looks, but whenever I met his eyes, he would turn away.

After we finished, Snake, Al and Alex were going to head into town for a while. James said that he was staying here to get some rest. I thought that was a good idea and decided to stay as well. I wanted to know what was going on with him. I figured it was something he did not want the guys to know about, but he would tell me. The guys left the hall and James and I walked back to the cabin in silence. The cabin was empty when we arrived, so I asked him what was wrong and he muttered, "Nothing."

"Come on, I know you. You always get this way when something's bothering you," I told him.

"It's nothing," he replied.

"It is something or you wouldn't be trying to hide it." I persisted.

"Piss off!" he snapped, obviously annoyed.

"Fine then, forget it." I went and lay down on Alex's bed. After about ten minutes of silence James finally spoke.

"You and Alex seem to be getting along."

"Yeah, he's a cool guy," I agreed, smiling to myself.

"I see." he stated in a flat, quiet voice.

"Yeah, why, what's up?" I asked, propping myself up on my elbows.

"I was just noticing how you guys are getting pretty close," he remarked.

"Of course we're close, we work together. We're friends," I said, laying back down.

"Friends," he repeated. There was something in his voice that made my pulse quicken.

"Yes, friends," I said.

"Friends who kiss each other?" he whispered softly, but loud enough for me to hear.

"What?" I asked, sitting back up. I looked over at him and he was watching me with raw anger in his eyes.

"You heard me," he said flatly.

"What the hell are you talking about?" I asked him, trying to hide the apprehension I was feeling. All I could think of were his eyes and his expression; a look I did not understand.

"I saw the two of you," he explained, never taking his eyes off of me.

"You saw the two of us, what?" I asked as my pulse pounded in my ears. I knew I was only making him angrier by simply repeating what he was saying, but I did not know what else to do. My mind was frozen. I felt paralyzed with fear, unsure of how I was going to get out of this and away from him. And I kept seeing his eyes.

"I saw the two of you kissing each other like you'd kiss some fucking girl." He practically spat the words out.

"You ain't seen shit," I was starting to panic.

"I saw him kiss you this morning. I saw him kiss you and then the two of you ran off together like a couple of fucking fags!" he yelled out.

"You don't know what you're talking about," I said as I stood up.

"Like hell, I don't." He looked at me with fire in his coal black eyes.

"He didn't kiss me," I tried to defend myself.

"Bullshit! I saw it with my own eyes!" he spat out. His eyes were beginning to water.

"I ain't like that!" I said, fighting the urge to throw up.

"Oh like hell you aren't! I've watched you at school watching the other boys. Why didn't you shower with us? You weren't insecure, you were just afraid we'd catch you jerkin' off. You're disgusting," he said, his voice laced with betrayal and pain.

"Oh, fuck off. You're just pissed off that I was actually good at sports and didn't need Daddy's money to buy my way into things," I said, edging my way towards the table he was sitting at. I knew I was pressing a specifically painful button of his, but I had no choice. I needed to get out of there before things became worse than they already were.

"Take that back." He stood up.

"Take back what you said, I ain't no queer." I was moving closer to him with my hands balled into fists.

"I never said you're a queer. Admitting something?" he asked mockingly.

"Fuck off," I said, turning away.

"No, you're right, you ain't a queer. You're a fucking cock sucker!" he yelled again.

I could not help myself. I spun around, walked up to him and punched him in the face. He fell right to the ground, cradling his head as he started to cry; I am not sure if it was out of anger, pain, or surprise. I was shell shocked and frozen in place. Disbelief flooded my mind as I looked down at my hand and saw there was blood on it; his blood. James and I had never fought like this before and this was certainly the first time I had ever hit him out of rage. I was shaking from the adrenalin pumping through my body.

Glancing back at him, I realized that I had broken his nose. I stood there, looking at my hand and seeing what I had done. All I could think of was getting the hell out of there. I sprinted to the road that headed into town and ran. After a minute or so, I slowed down and started walking. I did not care where I was going as long as I was getting away from the cabin, away from the accusations, and away from him.

Chapter Twelve

I must have been walking for about a half an hour when I stopped, sat down on the side of the road and started to cry. The tears kept coming and there was nothing I could do to stop them. I let them fall. I have no idea how long I sat there, tears falling down my face and my body shaking. I stayed there until a truck passed by and stopped. I stood up and started to walk again, until I heard someone call out my name. I turned to see Alex, Snake and Al all staring at me. Al called for me to join them, but I remained silent as I turned away and continued to walk. The truck started up and drove away.

As the sound of the truck faded, I heard gravel crunching behind me. I did not turn, even when I heard Alex call out my name. When his footsteps caught up with mine, I stopped where I was. I was terrified of how Alex was going to react when I told him what had happened this morning, that James had seen him kiss me. I was afraid that this was going to be the end of our relationship; that he was going to say that we could no longer be together.

I was barely breathing by the time Alex laid his hand on my arm and spun me around to face him. He asked what was wrong, but I did not answer. I could not find my voice. He glanced down and noticed my hand. It was red with blood encrusted on it. He asked me again to tell him what was going on, but I could not make a sound. Instead, a single tear fell from one of my eyes. Alex held my face and wiped away the tear. With his hand still caressing my cheek, I explained everything. I confessed that I had gotten into a fight with James and had likely broken his nose.

"What made you hit him?" he asked.

"He called me a cock sucker," I said, looking into Alex's eyes.

"And you hit him for it?" he asked in disbelief. He knew there was more I was not telling him.

"That wasn't all," I admitted.

"Well, what else happened?" he asked.

"He saw you kiss me this morning." I dropped my gaze to the ground as I admitted this. Slowly, I lifted my eyes to meet his. They were looking past me, not focusing on anything specific, just lost in the distance.

"What'd you say to him?" he asked hesitantly and I repeated the heated argument.

After I had finished, Alex gathered me in his arms and held me tightly. This certainly was not the reaction I was expecting. I enjoyed his embrace while it lasted, knowing that it may be the last time I felt his arms around me. After a moment, he let go and we started walking again. Alex turned off of the road and we headed into a field that bordered the forest surrounding the compound. There was a meadow full of long, wavy grass and wildflowers that swayed in the wind. We stopped and Alex lay down in the bed of flowers, deep in thought, picking at the blades of grass. I watched him, anticipating his reaction to James' revelation. After a moment, I sat beside him.

"I'm sorry," I confessed.

"For what?" he asked.

"For what happened, for everything."

"You did nothing wrong."

"Neither did you," I said, knowing that he intended to blame himself.

"I kissed you," he said quietly.

"Yes, but I made the situation worse," I admitted.

"You handled it better than I would have," he said. I sat there, slowly picking apart a wild daisy. It had caught my attention by swaying against my arm.

"Now what?" I asked quietly.

"I don't know."

"I don't want to stop being with you," I told him.

"Who said anything about separating," he asked.

"No one, I just thought that with James knowing about us, it might be better if we stopped..." I started to say what I was thinking, but I could not finish.

"We don't know that James knows anything about us. All he said was that he saw me kissing you. That's it and that's all he needs to know."

"But you know he's going to tell Snake an' Al." The thought of the two of them finding out was horrifying.

"Maybe," he said, deep in thought.

"Well, what if he does?" I asked.

"Just deny it," he answered.

"I already tried that. It didn't work," I stated, inspecting my sore hand.

"It will this time."

"No it won't, it never does," I muttered under my breath, but I was not quiet enough.

"What's that supposed to mean?" he asked. I had said too much and did not want to answer him, so I sat there studying the ground. My anxiety came back. I was afraid of his reaction.

He came over to me and pulled my face up to his. "It's okay," he said calmly. "Whatever it is, you can tell me." I did not want to tell him. I did not want him to know, so I leaned in and kissed him. He was surprised at first, but he welcomed it.

We sat there in each other's embrace and the familiar feeling of safety pushed the nervousness away. Soon, I pulled him down and on top of me. That feeling from the first night came back to me, the feeling of being one, breathing as one. This time it intensified. I pulled off his shirt and soon after that we were lying on top of our clothes, naked against each other. The feel of his skin against mine felt so good and I felt safe. I wanted to lay there, forever in his arms. We rolled over so I was on top of him and I just sat there looking down at him, smiling.

"What?" he asked.

"Nothing," I coyly remarked.

"Come here," he said. He pulled me down towards his face, caressing my lips with his. We embraced like that for a while, but I could feel him against me, his erection pressing against my tailbone. He was afraid to ask, but I knew what was on his mind. This time, for the first time in my life, I actually wanted it as well.

I pulled myself up and slowly moved back down with his cock inside of me. I was really nervous at first but once Alex was inside, I let out a moan of pleasure. Old memories and uncomfortable feelings began to return, but I would not allow them. This was different; this was with Alex, the man I loved. Yes I did love him, and at this moment I knew for certain that I did.

As I moved my hips back and forth, up and down, I could see the ecstasy on his face. I leaned down and teased his lips with my own. He returned my kiss with such passion that I was overwhelmed with pleasure. I finally felt complete. I wanted to stay in this moment of bliss forever, but I could not. I could not help but remember. I managed to suppress those feelings again and reminded myself that I was with Alex, forever and always.

At first, I was in control of our movements, but Alex slowly started wanting more and began to take control. I let him. In other moments of sex, he had always been hesitant with me in how he acted, but this time, he was uninhibited. He took over, moving me onto my back, thrusting deep inside me and looking into my eyes with a passion and determination that had pleasure pulsing throughout my body. Our climax was raw and powerful. The desire I saw in his eyes consumed me and I was trapped in the dark blue pools of his irises. I could see them when we were lying side by side, breathing and sharing our warmth with the sun glistening on the beads of sweat covering our bodies.

Alex broke contact first, pulling away to gather his clothes, keeping his back to me. I gathered my things and put them on slowly. I was starting to feel a chill from the wind. His back was still facing me when he broke the silence.

"Where'd you learn to do that?"

"Do what?" I asked.

"You heard me," he said flatly.

"Nowhere," I replied quietly. The chill from the wind began to penetrate my heart.

"Bullshit. Who else did you do this with?" he demanded. He was getting angry.

"No one," I protested. I could barely speak.

"Don't lie to me, Nathan. Who else have you fucked?" The only reply I could give was silence. "You said you haven't done this with anyone before," he said, looking hurt.

"I haven't," I defended myself.

"Tell me the truth!" he said forcefully.

"I am," I replied quietly. *Now comes the end of Alex's love for me* I thought. He would never look at me the same way again. He would never love me like I loved him. I could feel my heart slowly begin to crush in on itself.

"No, you're not! You've done this before!" he started to yell.

"No I haven't, not like this," I mumbled out, not realizing what I was saying. It was too late to take it back.

"So you have fucked someone else?"

He was breathing harder and was staring me directly in the eyes. I could see that tears were forming and from the tone lacing his voice, I knew they were not tears of sadness. His eyes were squinted and his brow was furrowed; I knew he was disgusted with me. It was the same look I had seen on my teachers when they asked me questions about my bruises and scars. That disgust was why I never told anyone the truth. Now the disgust was all I could see when I looked at him.

"No, you don't understand," I pleaded.

"Like hell I don't, you've been playing me all this time," he accused.

"No I haven't. I swear!" I tried to reach for him, but he cut me off.

"Whore," he spat and struck me across the face. The pain ripped through me, across my face and into my heart. I felt as though he had hit me with a rock. I looked up at him and he was sitting there, staring at his hand in disbelief as a single tear fell onto his palm.

The next few moments are still a blur to my memory, but I know that I stood up and ran. I ran as fast as I could, away from him, away from everyone. I felt myself leaving my body and watching things from a distance, a trick I had learned to do as a kid and had not done for some time. I heard him calling my name, but I did not look back. *Just run*, was all I could think and that was what I told my body to do. Alex chased after me, calling my name, saying that he was sorry and did not know what came over him. I heard him, I just chose not to care. The only thought that rang through my head was to run, and so I did.

Chapter Thirteen

I ran through the field towards the forest, entering it as soon as I found a clearing. Where I was headed, I did not care. As long as I was getting away from him, away from the look of disgust in his eyes, away from the shame for showing him what I knew, and away from the pain that was tearing through me. I heard Alex follow me through the field, but could no longer hear his shouts once I entered the forest. That did not slow me down.

I eventually slowed when I reached a clearing and then had to stop. My heart felt as though it was going to burst out of my chest, my lungs were burning and my face was hot. I felt where his hand had hit me and it was tender. It was going to bruise. I started to cry and I could not stop the emotions flowing through me. I could not hold it in any longer. I fell to my knees and almost collapsed entirely when I heard rustling off in the distance. I did not want to chance running into Alex, so I stood up again and continued on my way. I surveyed my surroundings to find out where I was and I spotted the gates to the cemetery; I had found my way back. I headed toward the gates when some twigs snapped behind me. Too close behind me, so I ran again with my legs protesting in agony. But I had to move. I could not see him; it would only hurt more.

I made my way along the broken road and through the stones of remembered love until I reached the angel monument; Shawn's guardian angel. I prayed that she would protect me and I hid behind her. I heard Alex come up to the stones of the small inner wall at the edge of the graveyard. He stopped, pausing for a moment, muttered something under his breath and left. I did not move from my spot because I was too afraid he would hear me. The angel would hide me for now.

Thirty minutes passed with no signs of Alex; my breathing slowed to a regular pace and I relaxed my body. I had not moved since I first hid behind the statue. My legs were throbbing, so I sprawled out and rested against the monument. As I massaged my legs, I tried to figure out what I was supposed to do next. I could not stay here. I needed to leave. Not just the graveyard, I had to leave the compound. Leave Alex. I had earned enough money to get myself to a new town, to start a new life somewhere. It was still daylight, so I decided to wait until nightfall and then I would head back to the cabin, grab my things and leave. I was going to leave and never look back again.

It did not take long before I fell asleep below the Angel's wings.

Chapter Fourteen

It was dusk. Only a few stars had come out and the sun was still shining light over the houses. I got up from saying my prayers before climbing into bed, my cowboy bed. Horses and their riders running all around the sheets, throwing their lassos onto a hidden cow that was just out of the patchwork. It was a gift from my grandmother. The cowboys were there to protect me from my night terrors she had said. She had given it to me on my eighth birthday, only three weeks ago.

As I jumped into my bed, I could hear my parents downstairs, their voices raised because they were arguing. I could not hear what they were saying, but it had to do with Daddy's after-work drink and how Mommy did not like him drinking as much as he did. They had been fighting about it earlier that day, too. I wrapped my pillow around my head and it drowned out their voices, so it was just me and my army of cowboys. I closed my eyes and imagined that I was on a horse with them, chasing after a group of Indians. My horse's name was Silver, just like my hero's horse. We were chasing the Indians because they had stolen our corn and we were going to get it back. Just then, my door opened and I opened my eyes to see Daddy standing there, his housecoat loosely thrown over himself. He came over to my bed.

"Did Mommy and Daddy's little fight wake you up?" he asked. His voice sounded funny.

"No sir. I wasn't asleep yet," I said.

"And why not?" he asked.

"I was chasing Indians, sir," I said proudly.

"Oh, were you now?" He got closer to me and I was having a hard time breathing. All I could smell was the bitter scent of his breath. He was drunk, and he smelt like it. I did not like that smell.

"Yes, sir."

"You're Daddy's little cowboy, aren't you?" he asked and I smiled.

"Yes, sir."

"And you would do anything for your Daddy, right?" he asked.

"Yes, sir. Do you need me to chase Indians for you?" I asked.

"No, son. You're such a handsome boy. I bet all of the girls in your school like you, don't they?" he asked, sitting on the edge of my bed.

"I don't know, sir," I said, confused by his questions.

"I bet they do, the boys too. Do the boys like you? Do you have a lot of friends, Nathan?" he asked, laying his hand on my cowboy quilt, where my leg was. I did not like how heavy his hand felt.

"Yes, sir," I said, still confused about why he was asking these silly questions.

"And do you play games with your friends?" he asked me, his hand still on my leg.

"Yes, sir. I do, sir," I said happily.

"You like games son?" he asked again.

"Yes, I do, sir."

"Do you want to play a game with your Daddy?" he asked.

"Yes, sir!" I said. I was happy that Daddy and I were going to play a game, but it was my bedtime and I knew Mommy did not like me playing games after bedtime. "Are we going to play a game tomorrow?" I asked him.

"No, we're going to play a game now. You're a good boy, aren't you? Always do what you're told?" he asked, squeezing my thigh.

"Yes, sir."

"Can you keep a secret, son?"

"I can," I said proudly. I always kept secrets, like when Jimmy at school showed me the dirty magazine he took from his Daddy's office. I was going to tell Daddy about how I am keeping Jimmy's secret, but then I realized that it would not be a secret any longer.

"Good. 'Cause we need to keep this game a secret from everyone, okay?" he said.

"Yes, sir."

"I mean it. This is just our little secret. You can't tell anyone, not even Mommy. Can you do that?" he asked, more forcefully.

"Yes, sir," I said. Now I was wondering what kind of game we were going to play that had to be a secret.

"I bet you could," he said smiling.

"Robert? Robert? What are you doing in Nathan's room?" Mommy was asking from outside of my room.

"Nothing Cheryl, just talking to my son. Now you go on to bed," he said, annoyed.

"Is he bothering you, Nathan?" she asked through the door. I looked at Daddy and he moved his head for me to say no.

"No, Mommy," I said.

"Okay then. Good night, sweetie."
"Good night, Mommy," I called back.
"I love you."
"Go to bed, Cheryl," Daddy said.
"Come with me, Robert," she said quietly. She sounded sad.
"I'll be there in a minute."
"Come now," she pleaded.
"I will, when I'm done with my son. You go to bed now."
Silence.

"Go, or heaven help me, I will make you go!" Daddy yelled. There was silence, but I heard her slowly walk towards their room. "Now, where were we?" he asked.

"We were going to play a game, sir," I told him, a bit nervously. I knew there was something wrong when Daddy yelled at Mommy.

"Right, now this is a special game. A game only Daddies can play with their sons." He moved closer to me. "Now let's get you dressed," he said, taking his hand off my thigh.

"I already am, sir."

"No, not for this game," he said, as he pulled off my shirt.

After he had taken all of my clothes off, he hugged me. All I could smell was the whiskey and it made me sick. I could not breathe. I could feel his clammy hands over my back, rubbing it hard. I did not want to play this game, but I was afraid to tell him, afraid he would get mad and make me cry like he made Mommy cry. He then laid me down and started to kiss my body. I knew that this was something only Mommies and Daddies do. I remember, because when Jimmy at school brought in his Daddy's dirty magazine, there was a Mommy and Daddy doing this. I was not a Mommy. I should not be doing this, but Daddy wanted to play. I did not like this game. He took off his robe.

"Daddy, I don't want to play this game anymore," I said and he started to laugh. "Please Daddy. I don't want to anymore."

I started to cry. I was getting scared. The look in his eyes was terrifying; it was like there was fire in them. He was enjoying this.

"Stop yer crying," he demanded angrily. His voice scared me, so I just cried some more. "I said stop!" he shouted as his hand came flying across my face.

The pain was unbearable. I stopped crying, afraid he was going to hit me again. He started to laugh. He turned me over and started to kiss my back. I just closed my eyes. I was not here. No, I was in a field, alone with my horse, Silver. A cowboy rode by and yelled out, "The Indians took our corn again. We need to catch them! Come on, Nathan, let's go!" I jumped up and climbed on top of Silver and rode away; away from my bed, away from Daddy, just away, chasing after the Indians.

Chapter Fifteen

I woke up crying. I was being held. It was him; it was Daddy and he wanted to play again. I started to scream, "No Daddy, I don't like this game. Stop, leave me alone!" I was pushing against him.

When I broke free, I looked over and it wasn't Daddy, it was Alex. My first reaction was to run, run and hide again, but Alex already had his hand on my arm, asking me not to go. He was reading my mind. He did not look angry any more. I looked in his eyes and collapsed into his arms, crying and shaking. He just held me and waited until I calmed down.

"Why did you run from me?" he asked, after a moment of silence.

"You hit me," I stated, making Alex pull away and drop his arms.

"I never meant to hurt you," he stated.

"But you did."

He held himself. He would not look at me, but I could see the pain on his face, the pain and the confusion. I knew now that I had to explain everything to him and that I was going to hurt him again. I moved over to him and held him.

It was late in the afternoon and had gotten dark. It was almost sunset. I must have slept for a couple of hours. After a few minutes of me holding him, he pulled away.

"What happened to you?" he asked. I looked away from him. "Please tell me. I found you asleep. I was going to wait until you woke up, but then you started to scream and cry. I didn't know what to do. I tried to wake you and calm you down, so I held you, but that seemed to make things worse. You kept pulling away from me." He became quiet after he choked out those last words. "Please, tell me what's going on."

"I don't want to," I stated quietly. I knew I had to, but it did not mean it was going to be easy.

"Why not?" he questioned.

"I don't want you to look at me differently," I explained, looking up at him. "I don't want to look into your eyes and see disgust behind them. It was there, earlier today, and it scared me." I turned away when I saw pain in his eyes. "I don't want you to be uncomfortable around me and I don't want you to stop talking to me." I paused to take a breath. "I don't want to lose you."

"You're not going to lose me," he assured me.

"I almost did," I retorted. I knew it was not fair to remind him of how he had reacted earlier, but that did not stop me.

"But you didn't."

"I've lost everyone else," I muttered softly.

"I'm not everyone else. I wish you would trust me enough with this. I want you to feel safe with me. I know that I hurt you, but I was hurt too." He stopped. "I don't know what to think, what to do. I just want to be with you. I want to know you, all of you, both your light and your dark. I've never felt this way about anyone," he said, reaching up to caress my face. His hand touched the spot where he had hit me, causing me to flinch away. "I don't want any secrets between us. I don't care if you have a dark past, I love you for you and nothing you've done in your past will change that."

I looked at him and saw something in his eyes. It was not disgust, but something else. What I saw in his eyes made me hope I could trust him. I took a chance and started to tell him everything, which I had never done before.

"When I was eight years old, just after my birthday actually, my father came into my room and did to me what John's father did to him." I said, as I pointed to John's headstone.. "That wasn't the only time. It never used to happen very often, only when he was drunk. But when the war started, my father drank more and I suffered more. He was too rough a couple of times and my back got cut by his belt buckle or his fingernails. You've seen the scars. I was never there though. When he came into my room, I would escape in my head. I would be chasing Indians, or wandering through a forest, or just lying there beside a creek, listening to the sounds of the water.

My mother knew what he was doing, but she couldn't stop it. One night she tried, but he just beat her. He beat her so badly I thought he had killed her and I ran away. I didn't get far and that just enraged him even more. That night, he broke two of my ribs. He would leave bruises all over my body from holding me down. No one at school knew. I was afraid to say anything, so I would always hide the marks. I never showered after gym class; I couldn't."

I stopped to pick a blade of grass in front of me. I was reciting this as if I were telling someone else's story, not my own. I was calm, the kind of calm you would be if you were just stating facts, not reliving the nightmare of your past.

"This kept up for a while," I continued, "until one day my dad got a letter in the mail and everything changed. He was conscripted; he had to go to war. He was gone for four years and those years were the happiest years of my life. I used to pray that he would be killed in the night; that a Nazi missile would fall on him in his sleep and he wouldn't come back, but they weren't answered. The day we got the news the war was over and we had won, everyone was celebrating. I wasn't. That meant he was coming home.

"But when he came home, things were different," I explained. "He was different. That first night, my mother and I were afraid he was going to start again, but this time I was ready. The four years he was gone, I had spent most of my time on the track and field team, getting faster and stronger. That night, I stayed in my bed, ready to defend myself or run if I had to, but he never came. He didn't do anything.

"That first week or two he barely left my parents' bedroom. He spent most of the time in bed, lying there, unaware of what was going on around him. When he eventually did come out, he didn't say anything. He could barely bring himself to look at me, let alone touch me. In fact he never did touch me and he never drank another bottle of whiskey. To this day, he hasn't had a drink. I was so relieved, yet I was still careful when I was home, afraid every night that he would return to his old self, but he never did. That part of him died on those fields in France, so I guess my prayers were answered after all."

I did not feel good, but I did feel relieved at having finally told someone. I looked over at Alex and saw tears falling down his cheeks. I leaned in to wipe them away and that made him flinch.

"So now you know why I know the things I know and why the smell of liquor makes me gag. Why I was terrified the first time we showered together, and the reason I fled when you hit me," I told him.

Alex was silent and I was nervous. I kept quiet, knowing that he would need some time to let things process in his mind. I stayed seated beside him, leaving enough distance between us, so he would not flinch away from me. During the silence that followed, a thousand thoughts of despair filled my mind. I was convinced that this was the end of us, that Alex would never want to touch me again. This thought caused my eyes to water and a tear escaped. Alex reached up and wiped the tear away. When his hand first touched my face, my initial reaction was to pull back. Instead, I pressed my cheek into his hand. He used that movement to pull me over to him. He wrapped his arms around me and held me in a tight embrace.

"I am so sorry," he apologized into my hair.

"You didn't know," I replied.

With his arms around me, I knew then that no matter what had happened in our past, from this moment on, we were inseparable. He was not disgusted with me. He was not going to leave me. I was going to have him for the rest of my life. This realization created a new wave of emotions that flooded through me, causing a new stream of tears to fall from my eyes. These were tears of pure bliss. I knew that nothing would keep Alex from loving me, nor me from loving him.

"I should have trusted you," Alex said once we had broken our embrace.

"It's not your fault. I could have trusted you, too, and told you. I didn't because I was afraid of how you would react. I'm glad I did tell you," I said, losing myself in his deep blue eyes.

"I'm glad you did as well. James doesn't know, does he?" Alex asked.

"No, he doesn't, and he never can. No one can," I explained. "Have you gone back to the cabin?" I asked. He nodded his head that he had. "How is James?"

"You gave him quite the bruised nose. It's bandaged. He told us that he tripped and fell. He kept staring at me though."

"So he hasn't said anything?" I asked.

"No, and I don't think he will."

"I hope not," I muttered as I rested against him and Alex wrapped his arms around me, holding and protecting me from the lingering nightmare that hovered in the air.

Chapter Sixteen

By the time we left the graveyard and arrived back at the cabin, the sun was just starting to set. I was extremely hesitant to walk in, afraid of what James was going to do, afraid of what he may have already done. When the cabin came in sight, I stopped in my tracks and stood there, staring at it. Alex turned to face me, blocking out the sight of the cabin and forcing me to look at him.

"Everything will be fine, just ignore him and things will be fine," Alex said, holding onto my arms. He gave my arms one last squeeze before letting go, turning back and started walking again. After a pause, I took a deep breath and went to catch up with Alex.

Walking in, we were greeted by Al and Snake as they were finishing up a card game. James was lying on his bunk and did not say anything when we walked in. He turned in his bunk so his back was facing us. I moved over and sat on the far edge of Alex's bunk, keeping my back to James. After a few moments, when the card game was completely finished, Snake stood up.

"What's the game plan for tonight?"

"We could head into town and go to Scooters," Al suggested, referring to their bar of choice.

"We do that every weekend. We should do something different," Snake complained.

"There's a band playing there tonight," was Al's response.

Snake still protested, but after some debate he realized that there really was no other place to go to. Al won and they decided Scooters was the venue for the evening.

"Hey James, are you coming? A little beer will fix your face up," Al called out to James. He rolled over, sat up and nodded his head in agreement.

This was the first time I had the chance to see his face and the damage I had caused. He had a bandage across the bridge of his nose. There was a bruise the shade of deep purple that spread across his face just under his eyes. He glanced in my direction and when he saw I was watching him, he turned away.

"How 'bout it Alex, feel like going out tonight?" Al continued his usual recruitment.

"I think I'll pass tonight," he said simply.

"Suit yourself. Nathan? Are you going to stay here and mope around with pussy-boy over there?" Al asked, throwing a pillow at Alex.

My first reaction was to stay with Alex, but I was feeling a sense of renewal. My normal apprehension and fear seemed to have left me. Knowing that Alex knew about my past and was still with me gave me a new sense of strength and purpose. I decided to test how strong his love would make me. When I told

Al that I could not wait to head out, the surprise that followed made me laugh.

"Alright kid, glad to see Alex's pussy attitude didn't rub off on you. It's only getting dark now. I'm going to shower and get ready. We'll leave in, say, half an hour." He left to shower and Snake followed. After a moment, James got up from his bed and left the cabin.

I went over to my dresser and started to undress. Alex walked up behind me. I could feel him there, feel the heat from his body, but he did not touch me. I think he was still hesitant.

"Are you sure you are up for it?" he asked, his voice laced in concern. I turned to face him, my shirt still in my hands.

"I know I was nervous about coming back here, but now that we are here, I realize that my fears were holding me back. My entire life, I have made excuses and told myself that I was protecting myself by not getting involved with others. If I did not get close to people, then they couldn't hurt me. Walking in here today, I realized that the only way someone could hurt me was if I let them and I refuse to let them. You've helped me learn this. The fact that you are here with me now, after everything that happened today is giving me a strength that I had never felt before or knew I could feel."

I reached up to his face and lightly caressed his cheek. He closed his eyes in response. Opening his eyes, he reached up and moved his thumb over my lips. We paused for a moment, before breaking contact. I did not want to risk being caught again. He turned to his part of the dresser and took out some clothes of his own. I watched him, wondering what he was doing. He laughed.

"Did you actually think that after what you just told me, I was going to stay here and let you have fun without me?" I smiled and we both dressed.

We were ready by the time Al and Snake came back from the showers. Al was happy to hear that Alex had changed his mind. James returned just as we were getting ready to leave.

Slapping me on the back, Al said, "Tonight, I'll show you a good time, kid." He laughed as we left the cabin, closely followed by Alex and Snake, with James ending our little parade.

We took Snake's pick-up truck, with Snake and Al in the front seat, leaving Alex, James and myself riding in the back. James kept himself turned away from us. Scooters was supposed to be "The only good joint to get a beer," according to Al. Judging from the crowd outside, it was.

Tonight was Swing Night and the band they had playing was certainly drawing in a crowd. Scooters was a mix between a pool hall and a bar. When you walked in, right in front of you were four or five pool tables which were often occupied by the same pool sharks. Then just past the billiards, there sat a mix of high and low tables scattered around the place. In the far corner there was a makeshift stage with just enough room for drums, two guitar players and a singer. Anything extra was placed on the dance floor in front of the stage. Lining the far wall, opposite the stage, was the bar which ran the length of the place. The stools were decorated with the regular bar flies whose expressions never changed as long as their glasses were full.

The place was crowded. By the time we found a table, Al and Snake were already drunk off of five beers each. Alex only had one, and he left it half full. I, on the other hand, had three beers and I still wanted more. Drinking like this was a first for me. Alex kept an eye on me and every time I turned to him, I just winked and smiled. I also went out onto the dance floor a couple of times. There was a girl who kept watching me. Al had noticed as well and said that if I did not go out there and dance with her, he would. I told him that if he wanted her so badly, then he should dance with her. Al just laughed and pushed me over to her. Even though I was forced into dancing, I still had a great time.

After our third dance, I was feeling thirsty, so I headed back to our table to get another beer from the waitress. Our waitress was a young girl, around my age. She had wildly curly hair and vibrant hazel eyes. She was tall with a proportioned slender frame and the complexion of a porcelain doll. She did not look like the type that would be waiting tables at a bar. She looked fragile, like she would shatter into a thousand pieces if you held her too tightly. She also looked nervous, like it was her first night.

When she came over to us, Al whistled and made catcalls at her, making me embarrassed. When she left our table, clearing our fifth round of drinks, Al, as drunk as he was, slapped her ass, causing her to jump and spill her tray. Beer bottles went everywhere, a few even shattered. This just made Al, Snake and James howl with laughter. I felt sorry for her, so I bent down to help out and when she looked up at me, she was crying.

"I'm really sorry about him, Miss. He doesn't hold his liquor well," I told her.

"It's okay, I've just been having a bad day and your friend isn't helping any," she said, picking up pieces of broken beer bottles.

"Oh, he isn't my friend, we just work together. My name's Nathan," at that, I stuck out my hand.

"I'm -" She was about to say her name when Al yelled out.

"Hey Nate, what are ya doin' on da floor wit dat whore?" he shouted loud enough for people around us to hear. I stood up.

"Watch what you say, Al," I warned.

"Oh, is somebody getting all pissed off? Why don't you just go back to dancing with your girlfriend out there," he said, trying to shrug me off.

"Take back what you said," I told him forcefully. I started to feel a hatred towards Al, a hatred that was not unlike the kind I felt for my father. It must have been the beer because I was also ready to fight him, as if were my father.

"No! Who's going to make me?" he asked me, standing up to intimidate me.

"Me," I stated, my voice surprisingly steady, given the fact that he outweighed me two to one.

"What the hell's a kid like you going to do? Huh? Nothing! I'll say what I like and not you or your whore is going to stop me."

At that, I lost it and threw myself at him, hitting him across the face. Once the shock of the first hit had faded and he realized what had just happened, he broke a beer bottle and lunged at me. Before he could reach me, Alex had stepped in and pushed him back.

"Get outta my way, Alex! I'm going to teach this brat what happens when ya piss me off," he said, lunging for me again.

"Leave it alone, Al. You're drunk and you don't know what you're doing. Just leave it," Alex told him, holding him back.

"Fuck no! Get outta my way!" Al snarled, shoving Alex.

"You'll have to go through me first. Nathan might not be able to fight you, but you know I can."

Al just stood there, glaring at me. I did not back off and I stared right back at him, keeping my eyes locked on his. Finally he looked at Alex, who would not budge, so he sat down and took another drink, muttering something under his breath. I turned back to the waitress.

"Are you okay?" I asked.

"I'm fine. I need to go," she said, pushing her way through the small crowd that had formed around our table.

The adrenalin pumping through my body was causing me to shake. I had never stood up to someone Al's size before. I was starting to feel light-headed and the stuffy air in the bar was getting to me. I went outside into the parking lot in front of the bar. As I was leaving, I was aware of Alex following me. Once outside, I could not contain myself any longer and I burst into a laughing fit. Alex grabbed my arm and pulled me to the side.

"Are you stupid?" he asked with anger in his voice. I continued to laugh. "He would have killed you, you know. Would you stop laughing and listen to me?"

"I'm alright," I said, still giggling.

"Why the hell'd you do that?" he asked.

"'Cause he was being an ass," I replied, annoyed. "And that poor girl was in tears 'cause of him."

"So you were really going to fight him?" Alex asked. He entertained the idea of it for a moment before starting to laugh out loud, making me laugh again. "I can just see it now…"

It was pretty funny if you think about it. Me, this average guy, slightly on the small side, was going to beat up a six foot, 250lb, ex-navy marine. Picturing that just made my laughing fit worse. People were coming in and out of the bar, looking at us like we were a couple of crazies just let out of the Loony Bin. I had fallen down, part from laughing too hard and part from the beer. Alex came over and pulled me up. I leaned in to kiss him but he pulled away.

"Not here. Let's go for a walk," he said. He grabbed my arm and guided me back onto the road.

Chapter Seventeen

The night air had heat pulsing through it. There was moisture in the air, making it thick, however there was enough of a breeze that it was not uncomfortable. As we were walking down the highway towards the compound, we walked in silence. It was a comfortable silence and the intoxication I was feeling earlier was beginning to wear off. The air was getting too warm for me, so I unbuttoned my shirt, taking it off of my shoulders and tying it around my waist.

"This'll probably be one of the last hot nights before fall settles in. It can get pretty cold up here," Alex commented as we were walking.

The sky was clear and the moon and stars shone brightly. I watched the sky as I walked and I stumbled into Alex a few times, which made me chuckle. He laughed as well, bumping into me intentionally. After we had been walking for some time, and were getting closer to the compound, I took my eyes off of the sky and gazed at Alex. He was focused ahead, occasionally watching the ground with his hands in his pockets. His shirt was also unbuttoned, but draped over his shoulders, leaving his glistening chest exposed.

He glanced to his side and saw that I was watching him. He laughed slightly, turned away and then looked back again to see if I still had my eyes on him. I did.

"Why are you watching me?" he inquired.

"What do you want?" I asked in reply.

"Why are you asking me that? You keep watching me," he said.

"I'm asking you because I want to know: what do you want? From me, out of us, that sort of thing," I clarified. He turned away from me and faced forward, staring at the ground while walking.

"I don't know," he mumbled after a moment of thought.

"Do you ever think about it? What we are going to do after we leave here?" I asked.

"Stay together," he said with hesitation in his voice; he knew what I was getting at.

"And do what?" I asked him.

"I don't know, I've never thought about it before," he confessed.

"Well, I am asking you to think about it now," I said. I stopped walking, causing him to stop as well. He turned to face me, and stared deep into my eyes.

"I want us to be with each other. Find some place to live and be together," He paused for a moment. "What's with the question?"

"I was just looking up at the stars and thinking," I said. I gazed up at the sky then down to Alex who had taken a step closer to me. I kicked a rock into the ditch.

"Well, what do you want?" he asked.

"To be with the man I love for the rest of my life," I said, making Alex smile. He reached forward to take hold of my hand. "Hey," I said, pulling my hand out of his, "who said it was with you?" I laughed.

"Jerk," he teased, pushing me playfully. I laughed and moved up to push him back, but as I tried, he placed his hands on both of my arms and held me in place. We looked at each other, into each other's eyes.

"I love you," he said earnestly.

"I know," I said. All I had to do was catch a glimpse of those sparkling blue eyes and I felt at peace, like I did not have a care in the world. I moved in and kissed him. "I love you, too."

We continued to walk in silence, holding hands and walking together, enjoying each other's presence. We stayed on the side of the road until we reached the rail yard. We bypassed the cabin in favour of being alone for a while at the lake. It must have been well past midnight. I did not care what time it was as long as we were together. A week could have passed by and I would not have noticed.

When we arrived at the shore, Alex laid down first by the shore of the lake. I followed suit with my head on his chest, his arm across my chest. We laid there in that position for some time, feeling each other's warmth, skin against skin until I got up and sat on his hips. I leaned down and embraced his lips with mine. We exchanged our love for each other with our mouths. I could feel Alex beneath me and I felt his hands moving down my back, slipping just under my pants. I loved the feel of his strong, calloused hands rubbing against my skin. They were the perfect contrast to my father's hands. It was wonderful. Every time his hands made contact with my body, I could feel myself pressing into them.

We rolled over onto our sides, still connected by our mouths, only now my hands were free to wander. I moved them up his back, feeling his smooth skin and pulling his shirt up along the way. His hands shifted away from my back to my chest and made their way down to my belt. He unfastened it and started to undo the top button of my pants. My hands traced down his back and slipped under his pants and boxers. The feel of smooth skin with the little tuft of hair at the top of his butt cheeks sent a surge of passion through my body. He had finished unbuttoning my pants and was slowly slipping them down my thighs. The cool breeze from the lake against my bare skin made my body pulsate with desire. I moved my hands from his back, across his hips to his lower abdomen, keeping them under his pants all the while. I began to undo his buttons and soon we were lying naked, our hard erect cocks pressing up against each other.

We rolled again so I was lying on top of him with my hands feeling his chest, my mouth caressing his mouth. My lips progressed down his body, slowly making my way to his hips. With my tongue, I traced the lines of his body along the way. After a mere minute of my mouth pleasuring his penis, he pulled me up and positioned me so I was on my back beside him. He then moved so he was sitting on top of my hips, as I had been sitting on his earlier and he brought our lips together again. He travelled down to my neck, only pausing for a moment, before he continued to make his way across my exposed flesh. He moved his tongue down my body, doing the same thing to me as I had just done to him. I never had this done to me before and my body convulsed with pleasure.

He found his way to my hips and paused a moment. He looked up at me and smiled before he took my throbbing dick into his mouth. I had never felt such pleasure; it was ecstasy. I told him he had better stop or I would not last much longer. He ignored me. It did not take long before I could not control it any longer. I came. The feeling was so intense, my heart stopped beating. I could not breathe and my vision started to go black. Never had I felt anything like this. Once everything subsided and I could breathe again, I pulled him back up and kissed him with such ferocity that I surprised him and he chuckled. While our mouths were connected, he was rubbing against me with such passion, he was shaking. I knew what he wanted. When I looked at him I saw fear in his eyes.

"It's okay. Remember, I want this too. I love you, forever and always." I leaned forward and kissed him.

I was staring into his eyes as he lifted my legs up over his shoulders. As he leaned his cock into me, pleasure flooded my senses and I knew that this was the man I wanted to spend the rest of my life with. We were connected to each other like this, with Alex's hips moving back and forth. His breath quickened and the passion grew more intense. I knew what was soon to follow. As he intensified, he took my dick in his hand and started to stroke it. We were moving together with such raw desire, I felt like I was going to explode. His breathing became heavy. Just as he started to climax, so did I, for a second time.

When we had both finished, he collapsed on top of me, shaking. I started giggling, I was so happy and he reacted the same way.

"That was absolutely amazing. I have never felt anything like that in my life," I said in between laughing and trying to regain my breath.

"That was amazing," he agreed, between breaths.

"You're still shaking," I said, kissing him softly.

Once rested, I felt a renewed energy. "Let's go for a swim!" I jumped up and ran into the lake. When I got up to my knees in water, I turned back to see that Alex still sitting there. "Come on, join me!" I yelled back.

The water was still warm from being heated by the sun all day. I turned just in time to see Alex land in the water right in front of me. We swam together, playing in the water and splashing each other for a while before I began to tire out. We returned to our clothes, put our pants on and headed back to the cabins to sleep. When we walked in, the guys had already returned to the cabin and were passed out in their beds. We both undressed and kissed one last time before I climbed up to my bed and fell asleep. The last thought that went through my head before sleep took over was that from then on, my life was going to be full of joy and happiness because it was going to be with Alex.

Chapter Eighteen

When I awoke the next morning my head was spinning, half from the alcohol and half from the sex. The other guys were dressed and getting ready to head over to the mess hall for breakfast. They barely spoke, beyond the occasional grunt of acknowledgement to each other. I was tentative about seeing Al, expecting him to still be upset over our fight the night before. He did not really react to me at all, and I did not want to press my luck, so I did my best to avoid him. James was quiet, like usual, only at times I would catch him glaring at Alex. If looks could kill, his would have incinerated Alex on the spot. Any time I caught James' eye, I thought I saw pain on his face and once or twice, when his guard was down, I swear I saw tears, but he would quickly look away before I could be certain. His anger was to be expected, so I thought nothing of the other emotions that were playing a game of tug-of-war in his mind.

We slowly made our way towards the mess hall once I was finally awake and dressed. Alex and I were the last to leave the cabin. As we were walking behind the others, Alex took hold of my arm and slowed his pace a little so we could talk out of earshot of the others. James did a side glance and noticed this, but continued to walk.

"We can't really talk right now," Alex began, looking over to James as he turned his head forward again, "so after breakfast, I want you to meet me in the washroom. Fake being sick and I'll come check on you."

"Why do we need to talk?" I asked, suspicious of Alex's impatience.

"Just do what I ask, please? It's nothing bad, I promise." I agreed to do as he asked and we continued on our way towards the mess hall. We caught up with the others and fell behind them in line for food. Al was first so he headed over to his preferred table that was on the opposite side of the hall from where Alex and I would always eat when it was just the two of us. We all filed over to sit with him. Snake sat across from Al and James sat beside Snake. Alex purposefully sat beside James and you could see James pull away. This left me no choice but to sit beside Al. He continued to pay no notice to my presence, but James refused to look up at me, even though I was sitting opposite of him. Any time I would look up and over to Alex, he would smile slightly. I believe he was getting some form of pleasure in tormenting James. I was taken aback by that, considering the power James had over Alex and our situation. All he had to do was tell Al what he had seen and we would be finished. That did not seem to faze Alex and I could not help but to smile in return because everything else aside, James's obvious discomfort with the situation was amusing.

We ate mostly in silence until Al and Snake got over their hangovers after about three cups of acid-like coffee. They talked and joked about "some dumb blonde" that was trying to pick up Al after Alex and I had left. The mood at the table lifted considerably and the rest of breakfast passed like every other meal the five of us ever shared. Alex's earlier request remained in the back of my mind throughout all of this, so I finished my meal before the other guys and pretended to look sick. I made a comment about going to the washroom to throw up everything I just ate, blaming the alcohol from last night. That had everyone laughing and caused Al to slap me on the back, which was his way of showing me that he was over our fight. I made it to the washroom to find another guy in there, washing his hands. I pretended to feel ill, again blaming the drinking from last night and the guy laughed. When Alex walked in, the guy was just leaving. As soon as the door closed, Alex had me up against the wall kissing me with more passion than I had ever experienced from him, so much so that I had to push him away just to breathe.

"Have you lost it? Someone could have seen you," I said, pushing him back. Not that I did not like his kiss, I was more concerned with the room full of testosterone-pumped guys just down the hall from us. "Someone is in a good mood," I said after a moment, sure that no one was entering the washroom.

"Last night opened up my eyes," he said with a smile on his face and happiness in his eyes.

"Opened your eyes to what?" I asked.

"To you," he stated simply. "Last night you asked me what I wanted from us. I spent most of the night awake in bed thinking about it and I came to a decision about it this morning. I thought about my future and I tried to picture where I wanted to be and every time I closed my eyes, I pictured a life with you. I couldn't picture a life without you. I love you and I want to spend the rest of my life with you."

I did not know what to do or how to respond to that. In fact, I was speechless until Alex walked up to me and wiped the tear that had started to fall from my eyes. That simple act of affection hit me hard and fast. I felt my knees buckle a little and he held me in place. The apprehension I was feeling seemed to disappear when he wiped the tear from my eyes.

"Say something," he said with hesitation.

"I don't know what to say," I choked out past the tears that were flowing.

"Say that you love me and that you want to be with me."

"I love you and I want to be with you for the rest of my life," I said laughing as I flew into his arms. I was laughing through the tears that were still falling down my cheeks. Once I had calmed down enough that I was no longer crying, I asked Alex what he planned for us to do.

"I have a few things to do in town, so I want you to pack our things and give your notice to the office. I will give mine before I leave. Meet me at the lake by sunset. We'll leave tonight. Don't tell anyone, they'll just hold us back," he said, with a glimmer of light in his eyes that I had never seen before. It was clear what he wanted. Yesterday I was ready to pack everything and leave, yet now Alex was asking me to do just that, except he would be with me. The more I thought about it, the more excited I became when I pictured living my life with Alex. It was quite clear to me what I really wanted.

"Okay," I agreed.

"If something happens, if either of us can't make it to the lake, I want you to meet me at the cemetery tomorrow. Wait for me, I will be there," he said.

"I will. I love you," I said as I snuck a kiss before we left the washroom. When I opened the door I nearly ploughed Al over. "Shit. Sorry man, I didn't see you there," I said passing him.

"You feeling alright, kid?" he asked me, his eyes locked on Alex's.

"Yeah those beers last night didn't mix with the eggs from this morning," I stammered. "Well, I got things to do. I'll see you guys later," I said, leaving Alex and Al behind in the hallway. I rushed out of the mess hall and nearly ran to the cabin. I grabbed the bags from under my and Alex's bed and packed all of the clothes from our dresser that I could fit. I was smiling so hard while I was packing that my cheeks were getting sore. I also could not help but cry again, only these tears were of pure joy and I let them flow.

Once everything was packed, I hid the bags back under our bunk. Once I checked to make sure I had not forgotten anything, I also checked the pocket watch I carried with me and it was 4:30 in the afternoon. I had about three hours until I was to meet up with Alex.

I headed out to the main offices and told them that I was leaving that night, a family emergency had come up. They said they were sad to see me go and gave me the money I had earned. I had not used any of my earnings since I first started working. I still had money left over from what I had saved as a kid and was using that on the weekends. I now had my bags packed and just over six hundred dollars in my pocket, not a lot of money nowadays, but back in the 50's, it was a small fortune to me. I was ready to start my new life with Alex. Things were going to be amazing once he and I left this place, and our pasts, behind us.

The problem now was waiting for the two longest hours of my life to pass by. I decided to head to the lake early and go for a swim. I was wired from excitement and I thought a swim would tire me out and help pass the time. I needed to distract myself from watching time creep slowly by.

It was a bright sunny day with a clear sky. The sun was just above the tree line, so I still had some sunlight left. I was not swimming to any specific place; being immersed in the water was enough for me. I was floating in the middle of the lake thinking about things, about everything that had happened in the past three months or so. I thought about Alex and when we had first met: the dark and sweaty stranger that had walked into the cabin and into my life on my first day here.

I remembered the first time we touched, while watching a movie on the hill under what we considered "our tree". The first time we kissed and all of those joyous moments came flooding through my mind as I floated in the water. Even the first time we made love, despite what had happened after, was a happy thought in my mind. It was the first time in my life that I had fully opened up to someone and they did not run away. I knew Alex and I were meant to be, I knew then that we were always meant to be together, to meet when we had, in that place and in that time.

I stayed floating in the water in this frame of mind for a good hour, just floating and reminiscing; I was there until the sun started to sink beneath the horizon of trees. I began to feel cold, so I decided to head back to shore. Alex would be here soon anyway. I reached the shore just in time to catch the last rays of light shining in the sky, and watched as the stars started to come out. I dried myself off, got dressed and laid down by the water, waiting for Alex to show up so we could start our new lives together. I knew I had left our belongings in the cabin, but I was too excited to go and get them and risk not being here when Alex arrived. I decided to wait for him and then I would run to get our things.

It was not long before I drifted to sleep. I was dreaming that I was a bird, free and flying in the sky, when I was woken up by the sound of footsteps, coming close. Thinking Alex was here, I got up to greet him. I turned around in time to see a fist coming at me. I fell to the ground and saw a shadow loom over me before I blacked out.

Chapter Nineteen

When I came to, I had a hard time opening my left eye. I felt it with my hand and it was swollen and tender to the touch. I tried opening it to see, but the pain was too strong. After opening my right eye, it took some time for me to adjust to the darkness. I could hear animals around me: birds and insects. I could also hear the sound of the lake and feel the sand under me. After a moment to get acquainted with where I was, I remembered what had happened. Someone had attacked me. My first thought was Al. He must still be pissed off at me for last night. I tried to get up, but my head was pounding and I started to feel dizzy so I sat back down.

"Good morning, sunshine," a familiar voice said.

"James?" I asked, focusing on where the voice was coming from.

"Yeah, it's me." Once my eye had adjusted to the darkness, I saw James standing by one of the few trees along the bank of the lake. He was casually leaning against it.

"What the hell? Why did you hit me?" I asked him, obviously pissed off and confused.

"That was payback. You broke my nose, so I gave you a black eye," he stated calmly.

"Shithead," I muttered.

"So, where are you going?" he asked after a moment of silence.

"Nowhere."

"Really? Then where are all of your clothes?" He asked in a patronizing tone. "I stopped by the office today. They told me they were sad to see you leave and asked me if I was leaving as well. So I ask you again, where are you going?"

"What's it matter to you?" I replied, annoyed.

"Well it would be nice to know when your best friend decides to turn his back on you and run," he said, trying to stare me down. I ignored him and held my head.

I realized something was wrong; it was late and Alex was nowhere to be seen.

"Where's Alex?" I asked trying to hide my anxiety.

"Don't know, don't care. Tell me where you are going," he demanded.

"Nowhere, now tell me where Alex is," I persisted, standing up.

"I said, I don't know," he said. He stood in front of me; his eyes were trying to pierce me, to study me. "What's so special about him anyways?" he asked.

"What do you mean?" I asked in return. The question threw me off.

"I mean, why him? *Why him?*" he asked forcefully, taking a step towards me.

"What the hell are you talking about?"

"Stop the act, okay. I know, Nathan. I know all about you. When you guys left the bar last night, I followed. I followed you two until you guys came here and then I watched. I watched as you guys fucked each other right over there!" he yelled as he pointed to the spot where Alex and I had made love. There were tears in his eyes. I was stunned and did not know what to say. "So why him?" he asked again, calming down.

"I don't know," I said.

"Do you love him?" he asked. The pain was clear in his voice.

"What does it matter to you?" I asked. I was losing my patience with him.

"I need to know," he said.

"Why do you care if I love him? I'm just a fucking cocksucker, right?" He looked down at his feet when I said that.

"Just tell me," he said under his breath.

"James, what's this…" I started to ask, but he came at me, throwing me off guard.

"Just answer the goddamned question!" he yelled, pinning me up against a tree and holding onto my shirt.

"Okay! Okay. Yes, I love him. There, are you happy now?" I asked in frustration.

Tears started to fall down his face. He leaned his forehead onto my chest, my shirt still in his hand. I heard him mumble something.

"What did you say?" I asked. He repeated what he had said, but I still could not make it out. "I can't hear you."

After I said that, James' head shot up. "Why not me!" he yelled. I just looked at him. "Why did you have to fall in love with Alex and not me?" he asked, his head falling back against my chest.

I could not believe what I was hearing. James had feelings for me? I did not know what he expected me to do, so I put my hands on his back.

"I didn't know," I said to him, causing him to pull back.

"Bullshit," he spat out. "How could you not know?" he asked, his rage building. "All throughout school, I was with you. I always sat right behind you in class, ate lunch with you, and joined all of the same sports as you. Everything you did, everywhere you went, and I went with you, just so I could be with you. Fuck, I even came to this shit hole with you, just so I could be near you and what does that get me? Nothing. Nothing! You have to fall in love with some other guy, some complete fucking stranger, instead of your best friend. Some friend you turned out to be," he said as he turned his back on me.

"James, I didn't know, seriously, I didn't. I'm sorry…" I started to say, but he cut me off by spinning around and kissing me. I tried to pull away but he held me there tightly. Finally I managed to push him back. "What the hell was that for?" I demanded.

"To find out what it was like," he said mockingly.

"Don't ever do that again," I told him.

"Why not? I'll do what I like," he declared, coming up to me. He moved in to kiss me again, placing his hand on my crotch. I pushed him back hard and he fell onto the ground.

"What the hell's your problem? I'm with Alex. Do you want him to kick the shit out of you?" He started to laugh. "I'm serious, he'll beat you senseless," I warned him.

"Oh, I don't know about that," he said in hushed tones.

"What do you mean?" I asked.

"Nothing," he said with this smirk on his face. I grabbed him by the shirt and pulled him up with my other fist raised.

"You tell me what the fuck you're talking about or I swear I will beat you so bad, no one will recognize you," I threatened him. I had every intention of following through with it. James just laughed in my face, so I hit him. I punched him right in the nose and let him fall to his knees. "Where the fuck is Alex?" I demanded.

"I don't know," he yelled back. Tears started to fall from him eyes.

"Where is he?" I persisted. I could feel anger swelling inside of me.

"I don't know!" Only after I stepped forward to hit him again did James finally give in. "Al was after him. I was just supposed to find you and keep you here," he said, holding onto his nose.

"What the fuck are you talking about? What did you tell them?"

"I didn't tell them anything." I took another step towards him with my fist raised, ready to strike again. "I didn't have to," he added quickly. "Al overheard the two of you after breakfast this morning. He said that Alex was holding your face and you said that you loved him and that you two were kissing each other," he choked out, another tear falling from his eyes. "He went on this big rant about how much he hates fags and that there was a fag in his squad in the navy. He decided that he was going to stop you two from running away together."

I felt my heart stop. I knew I was in danger and so was Alex. I had to find him fast. I started to leave when James tried to stop me.

"Wait!" he pleaded, grabbing my shoulder. I had had enough of him. I whipped around and hit him in the gut with everything I had. He fell to the ground instantly, holding his stomach, struggling to breathe.

I started to run. I needed to find Alex. We had to get out of here now, before it was too late.

But it already was. I reached the cabin only to discover that all of our things were gone. There was nothing left. I searched all over the cabin, but I could not find anything.

"They've been here, looking for you and Alex," a voice said from behind me. Jake was standing at the front door.

"Do you know where he is?" I asked. I knew I was panicking. I could hear it in my voice. He shook his head to say no. "Jake, listen to me, Alex and I are in danger. If Al finds us, he's going to kill us," I told him. He continued to stand there. There was something in the way he was looking at me, with pity and sorrow in his eyes that was making my heart strain. "Jake, please…"

"Hey, Nigger!" It was Al. I heard his and Snake's footsteps coming closer to the cabin, so I dove under the nearest bed.

"Hey, did ya hear me? Have you seen Nathan?" Al asked. I watched Jake's feet turn and face outside the cabin. I could not see Al or Snake from where I was.

"Who?" Jake asked.

"Nathan, the scrawny kid."

"Yes," Jake said and I held my breath. "He was with you two."

"No, not him you dumbass. The other one." I saw Al's feet come up and meet Jake's.

"No," Jake said. I could hear the anger in his voice. He did not take a step back.

"He hasn't been here?" Al asked, obviously ignorant of Jake.

"I said no."

"Don't get sharp with me, Nigger. He must be at the lake still. Looks like James is doin' what he's supposed to," Al said. I watched as he left the cabin. When I could not hear them any longer, I got out from under the bed.

"Thank you," I said gratefully.

"I didn't do it for you."

"Then why?" I asked.

"It easily could have been me hiding under the bed, being lynched for being black. Now, you had better start running because they were carryin' crowbars. When they see that you ain't at the lake, they'll be mad."

"I will. Again, thank you."

Slowly, I peered around the door to see if they had gone yet. They were heading towards the lake, about to disappear behind another cabin. I looked at their hands and Jake was right, they were carrying crowbars. The moonlight was glistening off of their wet hands.

I hoped Alex was okay. I wanted to find him and get us away from here, but I knew that I would not be able to that night. They would certainly catch me if I started running around the railway yard looking for him. I had to leave and meet up with him tomorrow.

As soon as they were out of sight, I grabbed a change of clothes and ran. I ran as hard and as fast as I could. I dashed out onto the road that headed into Lakefield and I did not stop running. I had to get as far away as I could. Whenever I heard or saw the headlights of a car, I quickly ducked out of sight, in fear it was them. I kept on running until I reached the outskirts of town. My legs were as heavy as lead, but I did not stop until I found the Route 66 Motel that was just inside town.

There were eight rooms all in a row with the office situated in the middle. There was only one truck parked in the lot and when I saw it, I panicked. I thought it was them, but when I got closer, I was relieved to find out this truck was green whereas Snakes' was tan.

As I was heading to my room, an ambulance and two police cars flew past the hotel with their lights flashing and sirens on. I prayed that they were not going to the rail yard. I prayed that Alex was all right, that he had escaped them and was somewhere safe. I also prayed that I would meet up with him tomorrow, that he would find me. At this point, all I could do was pray.

Chapter Twenty

That night in the motel was the longest night of my life. I could not sleep and it felt as if time had slowed down to a crawl. I was uneasy all night and my eye was still incredibly sore. Every time I dozed off to sleep, I was jolted awake by either the pain from my eye or from a noise outside. Every noise I heard, I thought was Al and Snake finally finding me. Among the twisted nightmares and fear, I fell into a restless sleep.

When I woke up in the morning and saw that the sun was up, I decided to get out of bed and I made my way to the cemetery to wait for Alex, as we had agreed. Getting there was not too difficult, but I had to keep my eyes open to make sure I was not seen by Snake or Al, or anyone else they might have helping them. I was not too worried about James seeing me, especially after the way things had gone last night. He would not have the courage to do anything to me.

There were too many cars passing by me that it was useless to walk on the road. I trekked through the ditch until I recognized the field where Alex and I had first had sex. I crossed the road when it was clear and walked out into the field. It did not take me long to find the spot where we had been together as the ground was still trampled where we had lain together. I only paused a moment before I followed my former steps into the woods and towards the cemetery.

By the time I reached the gates, I was covered in sweat and brambles from the bushes. Passing the gates, I felt my heart yearn with hope of finding Alex waiting for me. As I turned the corner on the road and the walls came into sight, my heart sank. It was empty.

Alex was nowhere to be found. I headed to the angel obelisk to wait for him. I sat down in front of the angel with her sword looming over my head ominously. I waited for hours, feigning fatigue and fighting off my imagination. It was creating reasons for why he had not yet shown up, each one much worse than the one before it. I was determined to stay, in fear of missing his arrival if I left.

I worried about him and I waited until it became dark and cold, but he never showed. By that time I had to leave or I would not be able able to find my way back out of the forest and into town. The walk back to town was insignificant and I barely remember it. I was starting to feel numb with every step I took away from the cemetery. *Where is he?*

By the time I made it back to the motel it was well past midnight. I was exhausted so I fell onto the bed and fell fast asleep. I had horrible nightmares that night. Alex was calling out my name, saying that he loved me, but I could not find him anywhere. I searched everywhere but he was nowhere to be found. I awoke in tears in the middle of the night. It took me a while to calm back down enough to fall asleep again.

I woke up the next day late in the afternoon. I was worried sick about Alex. I had not heard from him and he would not have just left without leaving some hint for me. Something must have happened to him. I knew that something had, but I did not want to admit it. I held onto some hope that he may still be alive somewhere waiting for me, looking for me.

After a quick shower, I threw on some fresh clothes, a shirt and jeans; what I had managed to grab from James' dresser before I ran. I decided to go to the town market to start my search for Alex; a search that ended at the door of my room.

As I was leaving my motel room, I nearly tripped over the newspaper left at the foot of my door.

I saw the headline: "Man Found Murdered."

I started to feel lightheaded and my knees went weak. I did not want to read it, but I had to know. When I unfolded the paper, I collapsed against the door, sliding to the floor. I could not breathe, my heart was racing and I was crying. There, at my feet, was a picture of Alex.

Emotions raged. Hatred, sorrow, anger, despair, regret, and then back to hatred and rage. I was so frustrated and upset all I could do was cry out and punch the door.

After sometime – I have no idea how long I was on the floor – I got up, grabbed the paper and headed out to a nearby park. I walked around for a while, unsure of what to do. A few things came to mind: I could go to the police, or I could go and find Snake and Al myself. What I would do to them, I did not know, but I knew I would probably die if I tried anything.

Many things went through my mind as I walked. The past couple of days with Alex, the first time he walked into the cabin, the smell of his hair, freshly washed after a shower, the feel of his hands on my face; it was more than I could bear. I found a bench and collapsed onto it, holding myself and crying. I was crying so hard that I did not notice someone calling out my name.

"Nathan? Your name's Nathan, right?"

I looked up to see the waitress from the bar. "It's me, Ruthanne. Do you remember me?" She sat down. "What's wrong, sweetie?"

I could not say anything. I just cried. She pulled me into her arms and held me close, causing me to cry even harder.

"It's okay, it's okay. Let it all out. You can tell me. You helped me the other night so let me return the favour."

Epilogue

Whatever became of Al and Snake, I do not know, nor do I care. I do not spend much time thinking about it because they are not worth my time or effort. I did run into James once, at a business function. He tried to talk to me, but I refused to acknowledge him. I turned my back on him, as he did to me all those years ago.

    I moved away from that part of the province and tried to make a life for myself. It did not work. I tried to be happy. I even got married, because that was what you were supposed to do in those days, but I was never truly happy. Ten years and two kids later, I told my wife everything that had happened. She tried to deny it, but I would not let her. The truth about my past led to our divorce.

I still see my kids every chance I get and I love them very much. Now that they have children of their own, I know they are happy and that I did not ruin their lives by leaving their mother. I had to leave her. I could not live with the lies I told myself any longer.

Do I miss Alex? Yes. Every moment I am awake and with every heartbeat. Sometimes, I wonder, at night. I wonder what my life would have been like if Alex was still alive. At least in my dreams, he still is.

I did not write this book to change the world or to start a revolution. I just wrote it so that you would know. Know that it happened and that he existed.

About the Author

Matthew Freake is an avid lover of books and storytelling in all forms, including theatre. He has won awards for set and costume design with the dramatic presentations of "A Gap in Generations" by Jerry Blunt and "A Bird of Prey" by Jim Grimsley. For the latter, he was also awarded for exceptional directing. He is also the author of the 'A Fairy Tale Murder' short story series.

If you liked this book, you may like some of our other titles.

To learn more about our authors and our current projects visit:
www.mirrorworldpublishing.com

Follow **@MirrorWorldPub** or like us at
www.facebook.com/mirrorworldpublishing

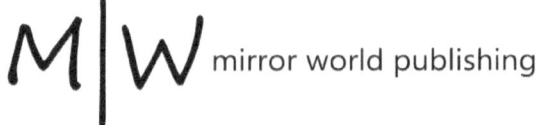

We appreciate every like, tweet, facebook post and review and we love to hear from you. Please consider leaving us a review online or sending your thoughts and comments to info@mirrorworldpublishing.com

Thank you.

www.ingramcontent.com/pod-product-compliance
Lightning Source LLC
Chambersburg PA
CBHW031423290426
44110CB00011B/502